Praise for Paul Ferrini's Books

"The most important books I have read. I study them like a bible!" Elisabeth Kubler-Ross, M.D.

"These words embody tolerance, universality, love and compassion—hallmarks of all Great Teachings. They turn our attention inward to our own divine nature, instead of diverting it outward. Paul Ferrini is a modern-day Kahlil Gibran—poet, mystic, visionary, teller of truth." Larry Dossey, M.D.

"Paul Ferrini leads us skillfully and courageously beyond shame, blame and attachment to our wounds into the depths of self-forgiveness. His work is a must-read for all people who are ready to take responsibility for their own healing."
John Bradshaw.

"A breath of fresh air in an often musty and cluttered domain. With sweetness, clarity, and simplicity we are directed to the truth within. I read this book whenever my heart directs, which is often." Pat Rodegast.

"Paul Ferrini's writing is authentic, delightful and wise. It reconnects the reader to the Spirit Within, to that place where even our deepest wounds can be healed." Joan Borysenko, Ph.D.

"I feel that this work comes from a continuous friendship with the deepest part of the Self. I trust its wisdom."
Coleman Barks, poet and translator.

"Paul Ferrini's wonderful books show a way to walk lightly with joy on planet earth." Gerald Jampolsky, M.D.

"Paul Ferrini leads us on a gentle journey to our true source of joy and happiness—inside ourselves." Ken Keyes, Jr.

Book Design by Paul Ferrini
Layout by Aryeh Swisa

ISBN 1-879159-39-2

Manufactured in the United States of America

the seven spiritual laws of relationship

A Guide to Growth and Happiness
for Couples on the Path

Paul Ferrini

Table of Contents

Introduction

This book is designed for people who are either in a committed relationship or want to be. A committed relationship is one path toward spiritual growth and transformation. It is not the only path, nor is it a very easy path. The seven spiritual laws discussed in Part Two of this book provide a roadmap for couples who are committed to their mutual spiritual growth.

If you are already in a committed relationship, you may want to start working with Part Two right away. If you are not sure about whether or not you want to be in a committed relationship, read Part One of this book very carefully. There is a great deal of pressure in society for people to be involved in a relationship at any cost. It is important to resist that pressure and make a conscious choice about whether you wish to be on a relationship path.

Even if you are ready to be in a relationship, you need to take time to get to know your partner and find a form for the relationship that works for both of you. By laying the groundwork for your relationship in a mature way, you have the best chance of establishing healthy patterns of relating.

A relationship is a birth of a new entity. It involves moving from an "I" context to a "We" context without sacrifice. This doesn't happen overnight. It takes time and patience. Clarity is needed. Both people must prepare for the experience.

A relationship cycle moves from birth through the apex of life to death and rebirth. Completion may occur through the death of one of the partners or through the agreement of partners that the relationship no longer serves their mutual growth. No relationship lasts forever. And many wonderful, important relationships last for five, ten, or twenty years.

All of us must confront the myth that being in a committed relationship means that we must be together forever. Every relationship has a beginning, a middle, and an end. The way that we end our relationships is as important as the way that we begin them. Part Three of this book deals with how we move from the "We" context back to the "I" context with gratitude to our partners for what we have learned together. It helps us to separate with love.

Relationship is the most challenging spiritual

path available to us today on the planet. No other path brings up our buried doubts, fears and insecurities for healing so definitively. It takes great courage for us to see the parts of ourselves that we have trouble accepting being mirrored back to us by our partners. Yet, by making peace with our partners, we make peace within ourselves and we come to experience our own wholeness.

Relationship is not just a quest for the romantic myth of happiness. That quest is over and done with in the first year for most couples. It is much more challenging than that. It is a quest for the Holy Grail itself, for authenticity in the midst of compromise, for understanding in the midst of pain. It is a shamanic journey with all of its unexpected twists and turns along the way. Sometimes it seems that our partner is more our adversary or opponent than our companion and friend. The face we see in the mirror is always changing.

The truth is that in the most profound relationships our deepest fears come up for healing. They come up because we feel safe enough with our partner to look at the shadowy aspects of ourselves and begin to integrate them into our awareness.

Not everyone is up to the depth of this dance. Sometimes we run away from the challenges of relationship before we have learned our lessons. That's why commitment is so important.

Committed couples stay together until they have learned all that they can teach one another. They know that they have reached this point when they can release each other with love, gratitude and respect. Anything less than this is not completion, but flight.

The spiritual principles in this book will help you and your partner hang in there through the ups and downs of your relationship so that you can learn and grow together. As long as there is growth and honesty, the relationship is healthy and is worthy of your commitment.

Of course, that doesn't mean that it's perfect. Even in the best relationships, doubts and fears continue to arise for both partners. However, couples on the path learn to hold those doubts and fears with compassion. They learn to be patient with and accepting of each other. That is what being in relationship teaches them.

As difficult as the journey sometimes seems, it

has breathtaking moments. The hard shell around the heart begins to crack open. Where fear used to hold us back, we learn to take little steps forward. We take risks, walk through our fears. We learn to trust each other.

We experience a gentleness born of the struggle, a sweetness born of the pain. There is a twinkle in the eyes that meet beyond the gravity of desire. There is an inner knowingness of self, of other: a surrender into the heart of acceptance and love.

May all of these blessings be yours.

part one

preparing for a relationship

Self Knowledge

Your primary purpose in this embodiment is to love and accept yourself and to extend that love and acceptance to the other people in your experience. You do not have to be in a primary relationship to accomplish this purpose.

In our society there is a great deal of social pressure on people to be coupled, in spite of the fact that the majority of relationships end in separation or divorce. Many people marry or live with people without being aware of the tremendous adjustments they will have to make and/or without having the communication skills they need to make their relationship work. This is courting disaster.

A more cautious approach to relationship would be well advised. Relationship must be a choice, not an inner compulsion or a capitulation to social pressure. We must understand what is expected from us and what we expect from others. We need to know what the challenges and the rewards of relationship are if we are to make good decisions.

We all have the option of living a single life if we want to. We do not have to marry or live with someone. We can choose to live alone. Such a lifestyle enables us to control our living environment and the overall structure of our lives in a way that would be difficult if we were involved in a primary relationship. It offers us solitude and the freedom to make choices without consulting another person.

A single lifestyle often works well for people whose primary commitment is to their career. They are clear that friends come second, not first, and they are not interested in developing relationships which would take time and energy away from their own creative pursuits.

Some of us are by temperament better suited to this type of life than we are to life with a primary partner. Others of us live with a partner first, separate, and then discover that we prefer living alone. When we know this about ourselves, we can save others a lot of grief by being clear with them about what we need. Then, if others want to be involved with us, they do so knowing that we are committed to living alone.

Knowing who we are and what we want in relationship is an essential first step on the path to intimacy. We can't expect to be successful in relationship with others unless we honor our own temperament and needs.

Fortunately, today it is easier to decide to be single without being shamed by our friends and family. Being single is a legitimate lifestyle choice. It doesn't mean that we are a failure at relationship. It just means that we choose to put most of our energy in another direction.

Learning by Living Alone

One thing that's very clear is that being successful in a primary relationship is at least as hard, if not harder, than being successful living alone. Indeed, you might say that success living alone is a requirement for success living with another person.

If you have never lived alone, you may not know what you need and want. Your experience may have been defined by the other people with whom you have lived. You may have lived your life trying to please others and win their acceptance or approval. Going from one relationship into another is not going to help you learn who you are. You may need to take some time to live alone, establish your own rhythms, and find out what's really important to you.

When you know yourself, you can be honest with others and encourage others to be honest with you. Then, it will be easier to find another person who shares your priorities in life. When you get involved with someone before you know your own priorities, you end up using the relationship as a foil to find out what you want. While that may be part of your learning process, it may also create unnecessary suffering for you and the other person. It's always easier to find out who you are by looking within than it is by looking at yourself through someone else's eyes.

Living alone is the best way to prepare to be in relationship. Finding out who you are, what you believe, what you enjoy doing, taking time for self-communion and self-nurturing, learning to love and accept yourself through the ups and downs of daily life — these are essential skills for finding peace and happiness. Unless you know how to experience genuine peace and happiness on your own, you cannot possibly experience them in a relationship with someone else.

When you know that you can live happily and successfully on your own, you don't feel a neediness or compulsion to be in a relationship with someone else. If you meet someone you really like, you are open to getting to know that person. But, if you don't, you aren't devastated. You know that your happiness is not conditional on someone else — anyone else — being in your life.

You stand on solid ground, anchored in your own life. You come from a position of strength. The people you meet can feel that. They know that you aren't afraid to stand up and be seen and heard. You aren't going to betray yourself for anyone else's sake.

When you are empowered in this way, you don't get into difficulty in relationship. You don't give your power away or take away someone else's power. You stand in your strength and invite others to do the same.

Coming from this place, relationship becomes a conscious choice. You don't have to be with someone else to feel happy and fulfilled. You can accept your life the way it is. It may not be perfect, but you know that you can embrace it. You may not be perfect, but you have learned to love and accept yourself the way you are.

Relationship as Addiction

When we feel empty inside, we usually look for something outside of ourselves to fill that emptiness. Sometimes the external stimuli is alcohol or a drug. Sometimes it is television, work, religion, sex, or falling in love. There are many ways to fill the emptiness, but none of them last. In the end, the inner emptiness just intensifies.

Behind that emptiness is a belief that we are not enough, that we are not worthy or lovable as we are. That belief must be challenged if we are to realize the truth about ourselves.

The way that you challenge that belief is to practice accepting yourself as you sit with the emptiness. When your doubts and fears come up, you acknowledge them and say "It's okay. I see I have doubts and fears. I don't have to be perfect. I can live with that." You learn to be gentle with yourself. You bring love to the dark, scary places inside yourself and, as you do, something shifts. The fears gradually subside or they are held so compassionately that they cannot run your life.

You learn to stand in loving relationship to yourself. When you do that, you come into your true personal power. You no longer need to look for love or salvation outside of yourself. You become the bringer of love. You take back the Self you once betrayed in the search for external acceptance and approval. This is a powerful act of self-redemption.

Until you learn to do this, you won't have a mature, fulfilling relationship. You will be using your partner in the same way that you use a substance — to temporarily cheer you up or alter your mood. You won't be facing the inner emptiness, the insecurity, the doubts and the fears. You will be medicating them or otherwise covering them over. This just postpones your dark night of the soul, the spiritual crisis you must weather to find the source of love inside yourself.

Even if you feel that you are on a relationship path, you must learn to live alone well before you commit to being with another person. You must face your fears and empower yourself. You must learn to love and accept yourself moment to moment.

If you don't do your homework, you won't be ready for the test. And relationship is the ultimate test of your ability to love yourself. If you dive into the water before you know how to swim, you will probably drown. If you become involved with another person before you have learned to love yourself, your hidden demons and those of your partner will surface and destroy the trust between you. So do your homework first. Meet your demons in your own consciousness. Learn to hold your doubts and fears compassionately. And then take the test of relationship.

Of course, whatever you do will be okay. Even if you enter your relationship unprepared, the worst that will happen is that you will learn that you were unprepared. You will have to go home and prepare in earnest. It's not like you won't have another chance to pass the test. You'll have plenty of chances. But you can save yourself a lot of distress by preparing in earnest right now.

Remember being in relationship is a choice. You don't have to be in a primary relationship right now. Maybe you aren't ready. If so, that's okay. It takes strength and courage to know when you aren't ready and to tell others the truth.

You never get in trouble by telling someone the truth about how you think and feel. If they don't like it when you let them know who you are, they will go away. And if they go away, they aren't appropriate for you anyway. The truth always protects you from others who might deceive you. It scares them away. When you are honest with yourself and others, you attract other people who can be honest with you.

Knowledge of the Other Person

Okay. Let's assume that you have taken the time to live alone and find out who you are and what you want. You have learned to love and accept yourself and to hold your doubts and fears in a gentle and compassionate way. What's next?

The next step is to be open to getting to know people as they spontaneously come into your life. You don't need to go out of your way to meet people. You don't have to go to bars or social clubs. Looking for a partner doesn't improve your chances of finding one. Indeed, the harder you look, the less chance you have of connecting with someone who is right for you. The very act of looking brings with it a certain consciousness of fear and lack. If you are looking for something, then you believe that you don't have it and that belief becomes a self-fulfilling prophecy.

So stop looking. Just love yourself, nurture yourself, do the things you enjoy doing. Live your life and enjoy each moment as if you were never going to have a partner. When you are tired, stay at home, take a bath and go to bed early. When you are feeling that you want more connection with people, go to church, to a dance, or on a group hike. Pursue your interests and your dreams. Take risks from time to time. Reach out — not just to potential partners — but to everyone. Cultivate friendships. Be visible and vulnerable. Let people know you and get to know them. Share your life with others.

It is in the context of sharing who you are authentically with others that you are likely to meet someone who is appropriate for you. But be patient. It isn't going to happen overnight. You have to be ready inside. You have to be complete with other relationships in your life. You have to be in touch with who you are and what you need. And you need to be relaxed about the process of connecting with others. The more pressure you put on yourself or others, the harder it will be for you to connect in a relaxed and comfortable way.

When you meet someone you like, don't jump into the relationship with both feet. Test the waters. Put one foot in first and then put the other one in. Verbalize how you are feeling. Ask the other person how s/he is feeling. Tell the truth to the other person and ask for the truth from him or her. Honesty is the cornerstone of any successful relationship.

Give the relationship time to develop. Instead of seeing each other every day, try seeing each other once or twice a week at first. Integrate the relationship into the rest of your life. Take the time to really get to know each other. Share your priorities in life. Talk about the kind of relationship you want. Find out what your partner's goals and aspirations are. Remember, you are laying the foundation for a good relationship. If you take care with the foundation, the building will take care of itself.

Be friends and companions first. Determine where your shared values and interests lie and explore them together. Look at your differences and see if you can accept them. Establish trust and mutual respect before becoming sexually and emotionally involved. Let there be an organic movement toward greater emotional and physical intimacy.

If doubts and fears come up about the relationship, hold them gently and compassionately within
your own consciousness. If they persist, share them
with your partner. Listen to each other without
judgment. Don't try to fix the other person. Just
hear what s/he is saying. Learn to hold your partner's doubts and fears in the same compassionate
way you have learned to hold your own. Realize that
it is natural for fears to come up when you go into a
relationship. Don't think there's something wrong
with you or with your partner when this happens.
Learn to acknowledge the fears that are present
without giving them power or making them more
important than they are.

Every relationship has its own flow. Try to work
with that flow, instead of against it. Listen to
yourself and to your partner. Find a pace that
honors you both. Don't push the river. Don't force
the relationship to be what you want it to be. Allow
it to unfold.

Inevitably, if you are enjoying each other's company and learning and growing together, you will
consider making some kind of commitment to one
another. You will also consider what form the rela-

tionship needs to take to meet your mutual needs and desires.

Negotiating the Form of the Relationship

In the past, we were given two models of relationship. Either we got married and lived with our partner for our whole lives or we stayed single. Anything else was considered sinful and was generally not talked about in public.

Today, we have many legitimate options for being in relationship. Having these options makes it easier for us to find the form of relationship that best serves our needs and temperaments as well as those of our partner.

The first thing that you and your partner need to decide is whether or not you want to live together and, if so, when that feels right to both of you. Some people feel comfortable moving in together as soon as their mutual commitment is established. Others need more separation in their partnerships; they may want to be together only on the weekends so that they have time to focus on work, family responsibilities and other friendships during the week. Still other couples live together but see each other only once or twice a week due to the disparity of their work schedules.

Some people want to be legally married; others do not. Some people want to have children; others don't. Still other individuals already have children who must be included in any relationship they have.

Some people want to live in the city. Others want to live in the country. Some like pets; others don't. Some people work a lot and have little time for socializing with their partners. Others want to share quality time with their partners on a daily basis.

It is amazing how many people get sexually and emotionally involved in relationships without discussing what they want and what they need in a partnership and a lifestyle. These issues are best discussed early on in a relationship when the friendship is being established. Then, if there are major areas of difference, they can be dealt with before major life decisions are made by both people.

While no two people agree on everything, it is important to have agreement on the major lifestyle issues. If one person wants to live alone and keep his life separate and the other wants to live together and share everything, it may be very difficult for the two individuals to find a form for the relationship that works for both of them.

Negotiating a form for the relationship that works for you and your partner is extremely important. It is an essential part of laying the foundation for the relationship. Don't be afraid to experiment with more than one arrangement if you aren't sure which one will work for both of you. You might try living separately first and find that you want to live together. Or you might try living together only to find that you really need to have more physical space in your relationship.

You can always change the form of your relationship when it is not working. However, it is far better to make changes early on when you and your partner can do so with a minimum of misunderstanding and hurt than later on when changes in the form of the relationship could result in considerable pain and struggle for both of you.

Once you have found the form of relationship that works for both of you, you are ready to consider making a conscious commitment to the relationship. This is where our discussion of the seven spiritual laws of relationship begins.

29

part two

the seven spiritual laws of relationship

The First Spiritual Law: Commitment

*A spiritual relationship requires
a mutual commitment.*

The beauty of each partnership is that it is unique. Your commitment to your partner does not need to look like anyone else's commitment. Whatever the two of you agree on is fine. You may decide that you want to live together or to live separately. You may decide that you want to be sexual together or not. If you are sexual, you may decide to be exclusive or not. It's all a matter of what you both are comfortable with.

The sacredness of your commitment to your partnership does not lie in its specific content so much as it does in its mutuality and in your willingness to abide by it. Your commitment is your covenant with your partner.

The first rule of agreement-making is: be honest with your partner. Don't pretend to be someone you are not. Don't make an agreement you can't keep just because you are trying to please your partner. Your honesty here will save you a lot of pain down the line.

A commitment does not mean anything if you can't keep it. Your ability to keep the commitment is what makes it a commitment. So never promise what you can't deliver. If your partner expects you to be faithful and you know that you have trouble being faithful to one person, don't promise to be faithful. Say "I'm sorry. I can't promise that."

Then, your partner might say "Then I can't be sexual with you" or s/he might say "Okay, I'll be sexual with you as long as you are faithful to me. If you sleep with someone else, will you agree to tell me immediately?" And this might be a request that you can honor.

Based on this interchange, the nature of the proposed commitment has changed. You aren't saying "I commit to being faithful to you." You are saying "I commit to tell you immediately if I sleep with someone else."

For the sake of balance and fairness in the relationship, the commitments you make should be mutual, not unilateral. It is a spiritual law that you cannot receive what you are unwilling to give. So don't expect a commitment from your partner that you are unwilling to make yourself. Unilateral commitments lead to some form of abuse or betrayal, not just for one partner, but for both.

When you make a commitment and realize that you cannot keep it, tell your partner right away. Suppose you commit to living with your partner and after a month of doing so, you are really miserable. You don't have the privacy or the quiet time you want. You resent the other person's presence and you find yourself being critical of your partner in ways that surprise you.

Don't be stoical and say "I made this commitment and I'm going to keep it no matter what." Shoving your feelings will only exacerbate your dissatisfaction, and you are likely to become even more passive-aggressive in expressing your discomfort with the situation. Instead, tell your partner that you need to talk. "I know that I made the commitment to live with you," you can say, "but I need to tell you that I've been having a really hard time honoring that commitment. I'm feeling resentful toward you because I'm not getting the space and the quiet time I need. I know that's not your fault, but it doesn't seem to matter. I'm blaming you anyway. I don't want to do that anymore. I think I might need to reconsider this whole thing. It may be that I need to live alone."

Your partner might not be too overjoyed to hear these words coming out of your mouth, but they may help him or her understand what's been going on for you. Chances are that your partner has been sensing your unhappiness and may be feeling responsible for it. When you own your feelings and tell your partner "I know it's not your fault. This is about me. I got in over my head. I underestimated the space I needed," your partner can stop feeling responsible for your pain.

When you ask to re-negotiate your commitment, you are basically acknowledging to your partner that you made a mistake. You are asking for understanding and forgiveness. You are asking for the opportunity to make a choice that honors yourself and the other person equally.

It is a spiritual law that you cannot honor another person by betraying yourself. Self-betrayal ultimately leads to betrayal of your partner, because sooner or later you are going to realize that you made a commitment you cannot keep. Better to face the embarrassment of that mistake than continue to make it. If your partner cannot forgive you, then you can work on forgiving yourself and being more clear in the future about what you need and want.

It doesn't help you or anyone else to live a lie. So don't pretend to be something you are not. Be truthful with yourself and your partner. If you make a mistake, say so. Commitments can always be re-negotiated. It's never too late to tell the truth. Sanity begins in a relationship only when both people learn to tell the truth.

This is not to say that we should take our commitments lightly. We should always endeavor to keep our promises. To do so, we might sometimes have to override a selfish desire and act with restraint. Or we may need to make the long term well-being of our children or other important people in our life a bigger priority than our short-term comfort.

We need to keep our commitments when we can do so without betraying ourselves. When we can't do this, we need to re-negotiate those commitments without betraying others. Our highest good is not necessarily at odds with the highest good of others. We can find a solution that honors everyone if we are willing to tell the truth about our needs and listen compassionately to the needs of others.

In the past, people made lifetime commitments before they knew themselves or their partners intimately. Since divorces were rare, those commitments often led to lives of mutual sacrifice and denial. People stayed together even though they were miserable. Obviously, this extreme of staying together at all costs is not desirable.

Today, we face the other extreme. More people are getting divorced than are staying together. People are not willing to compromise even in little ways to keep their relationships together. Many people leave their relationships before they have really given them a chance. Lessons are not being learned. Families are being broken up. People take the easy way out and then have to deal with the guilt they feel about their actions.

Commitments are serious business. Couples should be conservative and make realistic commitments. Marriage is not the only commitment available to people today. After three to five years living together, it might be realistic for a couple to be discussing a lifetime commitment. But a couple that has been dating for a year simply doesn't have enough information or experience to make such a long-term decision.

Nonetheless, it is not uncommon in our society for two nineteen year olds to be talking about marriage. That is not only unrealistic, it is asking for trouble. At nineteen, you don't know who you are and what you want. You have to take time to find out. At this stage of life, a commitment of six months or a year is more realistic. If things go well after a year, a longer term commitment can be made.

Even when a couple has been together for six months or a year, they should be conservative in making commitments. For example, it would not be realistic for them to commit to having children right away, since their relationship has not been fully tested. How can they possibly know after six months or a year if their partnership is strong enough to weather the emotional demands of being parents?

If you and your partner make an unrealistic commitment, there is a good chance that one or both of you won't be able to live up to it. It is better to make smaller commitments and fulfill them than it is to make a large commitment and have to re-negotiate it. When you shoot too high in a relationship, it can be painful to pick up the pieces and it may be difficult to reestablish mutual trust. Remember, small successes build mutual confidence and lead naturally to the making of more substantial commitments. So be conservative in the commitment you make to one another. Let it be a commitment that you know that you can keep.

It you commit to living with someone and you aren't able to honor the commitment, you need to look carefully at that fact. Perhaps you did not know yourself or the other person well enough when you made the commitment to live together. A more realistic commitment might have been to see each other every other day and on the weekends while still living separately. That would have given you a sense of what living together might have been like before you attempted to put your lives together.

Commitment is one of the most difficult areas of relationship. Without it, people don't feel safe being together. They don't know where they stand with each other. Mutual commitment helps both people feel safe. But that safety is not real if the commitment isn't realistic.

It is a harsh reality of life that many of our relationship commitments are broken. That's because many of us are over-committing or committing before we are ready. We need to slow things down and take the time to get to know each other before making agreements.

The following is a list of four progressive relationship commitments leading toward a lifetime commitment. The list is not comprehensive, nor are its definitions and timetables rigid. It is meant only as a suggestion or a guide to help you and your partner get clear on the kind of commitment you can make to each other. Please use this list as a springboard for discussing how you and your partner would define your relationship, where you stand on the issue of fidelity, and what timeframe feels comfortable to both of you.

Preliminary Commitment:
Developing a Friendship
(Non-exclusive/Non-Sexual. Timeframe: 1-3 months).

I will make time in my life to get to know you. I will also feel free to spend time with and get to know other people I meet. I will not be sexual with you or anyone else.

Intermediate Commitment:
Friends Becoming Lovers

(Exclusive/Sexual. Time Frame: 6 mo.-1 year)

I will be sexual only with you. I will see you at least twice per week while we both live separately and fully explore our relationship. I am committed to getting to know you as a friend, lover and potential life partner. I agree to tell you the truth about how I think and feel and I want you to tell me the truth in return.

Advanced Commitment:
Lovers Becoming Partners

(Exclusive/Sexual. Time Frame: 1-3 years)

I will live with you and be faithful to you. I agree to work out any problems that might arise in our relationship. My intention is to work toward a lifetime partnership with you. We share a vision about that partnership and agree on the major issues of work, children, location, lifestyle, etc.

Lifetime Commitment:

Partners Becoming Lifemates

(Exclusive/Sexual. Time Frame: lifetime)
I am committed to living with you for the rest of my life. I will be with you no matter what happens. Your happiness is as important to me as my own. We will make decisions together and be lifetime companions.

At each level of relationship, the commitment can be completed, renewed, or extended. For example, friends might decide to stop being friends, to renew their friendship, or to explore being lovers. Lovers might decide to stop being lovers, continue as lovers, or explore being partners. And partners may decide to stop being partners, continue to live together as partners, or explore making a lifetime commitment. Moreover, couples can decide to revise their commitment to a lesser one. Lovers can become friends. Partners can become lovers.

Relationships are dynamic events. Some relationships begin and end. Some progress to increasingly levels of intimacy and commitment. Others move to lesser levels of intimacy and commitment.

While it is helpful when we agree with our partner about the level of intimacy and commitment we desire, there is no guarantee that we will realize this level. No matter how careful we are about the commitments we make — no matter how well we know ourselves and the other person — we can't predict the future. We don't know what we will feel like when we move into another phase of intimacy. We don't know what fears will come up for us or for our partner.

There are no guarantees, even for those who commit to being lifemates. Every relationship involves taking a risk. We need to do our homework and make realistic commitments. We need to stack the odds in our favor. But even if we do this, no one can give us a guarantee that we will succeed. Our needs are progressive. We grow. We change. What we need and want today we may not need and want tomorrow.

Some couples grow together. Some grow apart. You can't know which will happen for you. When you enter a relationship, you enter a mystery. The result is unknown. You have to live it to know it.

Please be careful about the commitments you make, but don't think that a commitment is a guarantee. There are no guarantees in life.

When you and your partner make a commitment to one another, acknowledge that you are doing so consciously and with the very best intentions. But also acknowledge that you cannot give your partner a guarantee nor can s/he give you one. Understand that there may come a time when your partner cannot keep the commitment s/he made to you and vow to release him or her with understanding and love.

No one should hold another person against his/her will. Each person must have the freedom to commit and to end a commitment.

Freedom does not end when we make a commitment. In truth, we must have the freedom to revise or renew our commitment each week, each day and each moment if that commitment is to be authentic. Without the freedom to choose, we cannot commit. We can only capitulate.

When we feel that our commitment is no longer a choice, it becomes a burden. It becomes an empty shell. We stay together out of fear or guilt, instead of out of love and mutual respect.

This spiritual law is thick with both irony and paradox. If you don't intend to keep your commitment, then you haven't made one. But if you keep your commitment out of guilt or duty, then your commitment loses its meaning.

To commit is a voluntary gesture. It is an act of free will. When it ceases to be free and voluntary, it no longer means anything. You can't hold other people to promises they cannot fulfill. To do so only creates suffering for them and for you.

Freedom must always be the other side of commitment. If you can't set your partner free from the commitment s/he makes to you, don't ask for that commitment. Your job is not to bind your partner to the promises of the past, but to gratefully receive his/her commitment as an act of free will in this moment.

If there is even a hint of coercion in the way you hold your partner's commitment, you will be sowing the seeds of resentment and discord. Keep setting your partner free so that s/he can continue to commit to you in good faith now and in the future.

It is a spiritual law that you can have only what you are prepared to give up. The more you surrender the gift, the more it can be given to you.

The Second Spiritual Law: Sharing

A spiritual relationship requires
regular sharing between partners.

It is very difficult to have a primary relationship with a person who does not share your vision of relationship, your values, your lifestyle goals, your interests and your way of being. Before you consider getting seriously involved with someone, it is important to know that you enjoy each other, respect each other and have many areas of life to share together.

In the romantic phase of a relationship, differences are tolerated and similarities are emphasized. Both people are working hard to please and accommodate each other. When mutual desire is at its apex, people who are very different can get along without great difficulty. But the romantic phase does not last forever. People get more familiar with one another. They cease to be on their good behavior. They stop trying to please each other. They start to reveal themselves more authentically. Unconscious habits and tendencies surface. Fears, doubts, and anxieties arise about self and other. As the expression goes "The honeymoon is over."

The romantic phase brings people together. When it ends, people frequently move apart. Sometimes, they even feel betrayed by one another.

In truth, the spiritual aspect of the relationship does not begin until the couple weathers the death of their romance. Then, when they look at each other (without stars in their eyes), do they like what they see? Can they look at their partner's dark side and accept it in the same compassionate way that they learn to accept their own? Are they looking for another human being or a saint?

Realism inevitably replaces romanticism. In this new phase of relationship, we are challenged to accept our partner just the way s/he is. We aren't going to be able to change or redeem this person. We aren't going to be able to remake him or her to fit the image of what we think a partner should be. We have to face the reality of how our partner is right now. Can we accept that?

No partner is perfect. No partner is going to measure up to all our expectations and fantasies. From the perspective of our ego, any partner would be found wanting. The question is: can we go beyond our ego perspective? Can we learn to love and accept the imperfect person who stands before us, who in so many ways is a mirror of ourselves?

Some people never make it into phase two of relationship. They are addicted to romance. When one romance ends, they find another. They like being pumped up.

Falling in love is truly like a drug. It makes you very high for a short period of time, but inevitably you crash. Then, if you are an addict, you go out and get another fix. You find another woman or man to fall in love with and you lose yourself in each other.

You don't have to have that much in common to fall in love. When you are high, it seems as if you could share anything with your partner. It's only when the drug wears off that you realize that you and this other person may not have very much in common. It can be very painful to look at someone whose bed you have been sharing for three or four months and realize that you have very different values, interests, and goals in life.

Everyone likes falling in love. Who wouldn't like a hormone rush? But very few people realize how dangerous it can be. I hate to say this — because it bursts everyone's bubble, including my own — but it is true: falling in love is the greatest single obstacle to genuine partnership. Very few couples survive it. The ones who do survive are the ones who either took the time to get to know each other before they fell in love or the ones who were just plain lucky.

When romance is over, what you have left is what is real and grounded: the way you live, the kind of work you do, the kind of thoughts you think, the way you spend your spare time, the challenges you accept, the fears that come up for you. If you have a partner who enjoys a similar lifestyle, similar interests, and similar aspirations, then you have a good chance of making it in phase two of the relationship. If you don't have such a partner, don't be surprised if phase two lasts only for a week or a month. Then, the next time you are about to fall in love, ask yourself "Do I really know this person? Is this someone I can share my life with?" And if the answer is "No," or "I don't know," then ask for a friendship first so that the two of you can get to know each other.

Phase two of relationship has to do with accepting each other's strengths and weaknesses, dark side and bright side, hopes and fears. In many ways, this is the dark night of the soul of relationship — the time when you must confront your partner's humanness and your own. It is the opposite of phase one. There is nothing romantic about it.

Having a foundation of common interests, shared vision and values makes it possible for you to face the imperfection in yourself, your partner and your relationship without giving up hope. You are able to hang in there together as friends, not just as lovers. You develop respect for each other and learn to forgive each other's mistakes. You develop genuine compassion for one another.

Until you reach this point with your partner, you haven't established your relationship as a spiritual reality. You haven't gone beyond your mutual ego needs into the heart of love and acceptance.

If your goal is to have a lasting, spiritually uplifting relationship, you would do well to be sure that you and your partner have a shared vision of your relationship, shared values and beliefs, shared interests, and a shared commitment to being together.

Let's look briefly at each one of these areas.

1. Shared Vision

A shared vision means that you and your partner agree on what's important in your relationship and where you would like it to go. Often, it is helpful to articulate your shared vision in writing and to revise it whenever necessary. A helpful ritual is to review this vision statement every year at the anniversary of your relationship.

2. Shared Values

Your values are the moral code you live by. You know what you think is right and what you think is wrong, what is acceptable and what is not acceptable to you. You may believe in legal marriage or you may not. You may value fidelity, freedom of thought, honesty, consistency, cleanliness, open-mindedness. You fill in the blanks. Perhaps you have religious, philosophical, or political views that you would need to share with a partner. You may be committed to being a vegetarian. You might believe in abstaining from alcohol or drugs. You may be passionate about human rights. Get clear on what's most important to you and share this with your potential partner. While the two of you are not likely to agree on all values, it is important that you agree on the values that are most significant to each of you.

3. Shared Interests

Your interests are the things that you like to do. You might like to read historical novels, watch basketball, go hiking, listen to jazz or classical music, go dancing, or take trips to exotic places. You might spend a lot of your time watching television or surfing the Internet. You may like to take week-long expeditions into the mountains or the deep forest. Working out every day may be a priority for you or it may not.

Obviously, you and your partner are not going to share all or even most of the same interests. But it is important that you do share at least two or three interests that are important to both of you.

Pursuing your interests and hobbies is essential to the quality of your life. It puts a strain on your relationship when you and your partner are always doing things separately. You don't have time to connect and enjoy each other's company.

Of course, your interests aren't static, nor are your partner's. Both of you will be exploring new subjects and new activities. It is important to make an effort to explore some of these together. While neither one of you might feel passionate about going to the theater or taking a computer course, it may be enjoyable for both of you. It enables you to connect in new ways. It helps you build a shared experience together.

Just as it is appropriate for you to pursue individually an interest that your partner does not share, it is equally appropriate that you find areas where you and your partner can participate together. Successful relationships have a rich, varied area of shared experience. That shared experience gives the relationship the strength it needs to support the freedom of each partner to pursue separate interests and hobbies.

Some couples need to share a great deal to feel connected. Others need to have a lot of space to pursue their separate interests and agendas. As long as there is mutuality here, there is no problem. Hopefully, you did your homework and chose a partner whose need for sharing is compatible with your own. If not, you will have some important negotiation to do in this area.

You and your partner should plan to build into your life specific times for sharing and connecting with each other. Each day, for example, the two of you might agree to take fifteen minutes to share thoughts and feelings, massage each other, meditate together, cook and eat together, or take an evening walk together. Once a week the two of you might go out to dinner, to church, or get together with mutual friends. Once every month or two you might go on a special hike or take a weekend trip. And once a year you might take a week and go on retreat together or take a vacation to celebrate your relationship.

By ritualizing your shared time, you make sure that you feed the relationship on a regular basis. If you leave shared time to chance, you will find that there aren't as many chances as you thought there would be. Each of you will get involved in your separate lives and you may wake up one day to find that you have grown apart.

4. Shared Lifestyle

Your lifestyle consists of where and how you want to live. Do you want to live in the city or the country, in an apartment or a house? Do you live with children or want to have them? Do you like pets or dislike them? Do you eat meat and potatoes or organic foods? Do you live on $10,000 a year, drive a used car, and make your own clothes, or do you make $100,000 a year, drive a brand new car, and buy expensive clothes?

Lifestyle issues make up a good deal of the success or failure of relationships, especially when people live together. Lack of agreement on the most important of these issues can prevent a relationship from developing to its full potential.

5. Shared Commitment

The issue of shared commitment has been discussed already. Unlike the other areas of sharing, where differences can and must be tolerated, mutual agreement is essential here. Every couple must take time to periodically evaluate the issue of commitment and make revisions if necessary. Commitment is like the rudder on a boat. Without a clear, strong mutual commitment, your relationship will be set adrift on the sea of life without purpose or direction.

The Third Spiritual Law: Growth

In a spiritual relationship, both people must be free to grow and express themselves as individuals.

Differences are as important as similarities in a relationship. It's easy to love people who agree with us and share our values and interests. It's not so easy to love people who disagree with us and have very different values and interests. To do this, we must love unconditionally. Our love must be based on acceptance, not on agreement.

In any relationship there will be times when we do not agree with our partners. When we disagree with them, do we do so with love and respect? Do we honor our differences, or do we resist them? Do we try to change our partner's ideas or do we accept them? Do we accept our own ideas or do we try to change them so that our partner will accept us?

A spiritual partnership is based on unconditional love and acceptance. We don't have to agree with our partners to love and accept them. We don't have to do everything together to feel connected to our partners. We can give our partners the space to be themselves.

Boundary issues are extremely important in relationship. The fact that we are coupled does not mean that we cease to be individuals. Couples who become enmeshed and co-dependent are sowing the seeds of future discord. No one should give up being himself to be with another person. In fact, the strength of a relationship can be measured by the degree to which each partner feels free to self-actualize within the context of the partnership.

When everything needs to be shared, sharing becomes a compulsion, not a voluntary act. Only a very insecure person needs to do everything with his or her partner. A secure person gives his or her partner freedom to be who s/he is.

Growth and sharing are equally important in a relationship. Sharing promotes stability and a feeling of closeness. Growth promotes learning and expansion of consciousness.

A relationship that does not allow for individual differences and the freedom to pursue separate interests closes in on itself. Both partners feel stultified, held back, controlled, or in a rut. When neither partner is growing and self-actualizing, no new energy is brought into the relationship and it stagnates. Couples interact in predictable ways. They take each other for granted. They don't challenge one another. There is no excitement or mystery in the relationship.

This is one relationship extreme. Here, the security needs of both partners predominate over their growth needs. A relationship that continues in this mode may feel safe, secure and predictable, but it lacks energy, excitement, and challenge. One or both partners may have affairs in an effort to rediscover challenge and excitement in their lives. But going outside of the relationship for stimulation doesn't address the need for internal changes in the relationship.

Couples can avoid stagnation in their relationship by encouraging one another to pursue interests that are not shared. By having separate interests and friendships, each person brings new energy back to the relationship. If a couple has a strong enough base of sharing and commitment, they can grant each other this kind of freedom without feeling jealous of or competitive with one another.

Of course, the other relationship extreme is when the growth needs of both partners predominate over their security needs. In such a relationship, couples spend very little time sharing together. They lead very independent lives, pursuing many outside interests and friendships. Such relationships are very stimulating because there is always new energy coming back into the relationship. But they lack stability and nurturing. Without a strong foundation of shared time and experience, each partner can be easily threatened by the other person's outside friendships, interests and career commitments.

When security needs dominate in a relationship the danger is emotional stagnation and creative frustration. When growth needs dominate, the danger is emotional instability or disconnection and lack of trust.

Moreover, in some relationships one partner is the stable, secure one who holds the relationship together, and the other is the restless, risk-taking one pursuing new growth experiences. In such cases, one partner grows faster than the other and often gets bored with the relationship. Unless the other partner opens to new growth experiences, the relationship may become untenable.

To avoid these potential problems, you and your

partner need to look carefully at your individual growth needs. Are you giving each other enough space to grow as individuals? Are you encouraging one another to pursue your individual dreams and creative interests?

Ask yourself as an individual "Am I committed to my own growth, creative expression and self-actualization? Am I taking the steps I need to take to grow and express myself as a person?" or "Am I trying to find meaning in life exclusively in the relationship with my partner?"

Couples who try to live their entire lives through each other are asking for trouble. The old adage "familiarity breeds contempt" has some measure of truth to it. Couples who spend too much time together are putting impossible pressure on their relationship. While a primary relationship can be a major source of meaning and fulfillment for a person, it can't be the sole source. Each person must find some meaning and fulfillment in self-defined and self-initiated activities, as well as in interpersonal relationships that don't involve the primary partner.

You and your partner need to determine where

you stand on the sharing/growth continuum. Are you in agreement about how much sharing and alone time you both need? If not, can you find a way to bridge the gap? Shared time needs to be sufficient to enable the "security-oriented" partner to support the "growth-oriented" partner in pursuing interests and friendships outside of the relationship? And the latter must make a conscious attempt to share his or her outside experience with the "security-oriented" partner, so that there are no secrets which erode trust.

The following worksheet may help you and your partner begin to get a handle on these issues.

Worksheet for Sharing and Growth Commitments

Part One: Sharing

1. List the interests and activities that you want to share with your partner. Be sure to include the obvious ones such as eating together and making love.

2. From this list, choose one or more areas you want to share on a daily basis, a weekly

basis, every month or two, and at least once per year.

3. Share your list with your partner. Ask your partner to share his or her list with you. Determine where you are in agreement and where you are not in agreement.

4. Make a plan for sharing based on the interests and activities that are important to both of you, and see if it can include at least one interest or activity that is important to one of you and acceptable to the other.

Part Two: Growth

1. Make a list of the interests and areas of creative expression that are important to you and that your partner cannot or does not wish to share with you.

2. Which of these interests/activities are you committed to pursuing by yourself on a daily basis, a weekly basis, once every month or two, at least once per year?

3. Ask your partner if s/he is willing to support you in pursuing these interests/ activities on your own. Ask your partner to

share his/her list with you and let your partner know how you could support him/her.

4. Make a plan for pursuing these important interests/activities with your partner's encouragement and support.

5. Encourage your partner to make a plan for pursuing the activities/interests that are important to him or her.

Once you and your partner develop a plan for sharing and growth, you will need to test it out to see where it works and where it doesn't. If you overestimated the amount of time available to you for all of these activities, you might have to consider cutting back on your commitments. If too much emphasis is going to growth and you are feeling disconnected from each other, you may need to re-emphasize shared time and activities. If you are both feeling that you don't have enough alone time, you may have to re-emphasize growth activities. If you disagree about how the plan is working, you might need to re-negotiate it.

The reason to do this exercise is not to avoid making mistakes, but to bring into your conscious awareness the potential problems for both of you. These problems will surface sooner or later in the relationship and it is easier to deal with them in a context of mutual exploration than in a context of mutual disappointment and betrayal.

Sharing is essential in a primary relationship. But no relationship, no matter how outstanding, can satisfy all of the growth needs of both partners. Each person must take responsibility for growing, changing, expressing self, and expanding in consciousness.

It is always tempting when we first get involved with someone to think that the relationship is going to make us happy. But that is a dangerous thought. If we are not taking responsibility for our own happiness, then who is? The answer is "No one."

We can't expect our partners to take care of our needs for growth and creative self-expression. They must take care of their own needs in this respect.

It is up to each one of us to say what we need and be committed to it. If our partner opposes our plan for self-actualization, that is an important sign that the relationship may not be right for us. Regardless of how much we have in common with our partner, we need to pursue our own goals and dreams. If our partner cannot support us in this way, we may have to draw the line and back away from our commitment to that person.

Not only do we offer our partners the gift of our commitment, we also offer them the gift of freedom. And they offer us the same two gifts. One gift without the other doesn't mean anything. We can't be committed to our partners if we don't have the freedom to be ourselves. And our partners cannot be committed to us if they don't have our blessing to pursue their goals and dreams.

Growth is not only essential for each individual; it is also essential for the relationship itself. Couples would do well to engage occasionally in activities that challenge the relationship to deepen in intimacy and trust. They can do this in a variety of ways: by going to counseling together, by attending a couples workshop, by taking a wilderness expedition together, or by attending a spiritual retreat. Any type of activity that breaks the routine of the couple and helps the individuals involved see each other in new ways is growth enhancing.

The relationship between growth and sharing is

a powerful one. It is most dynamic when there is sufficient trust and freedom in a relationship to enable both partners to explore their separate dreams and when there is mutual willingness to share those individual growth experiences with the partner. Then, sharing and growth are not at odds, but actually complement one another and help to keep the relationship energetically vital and emotionally healthy.

Couples will need to constantly review the balance between growth and sharing in their relationship. This balance changes over time, as the needs of each partner and the needs of the relationship itself change. There may be times when growth is accentuated and sharing is at a minimum and that may be acceptable to both people. There may be times when sharing and nurturing are the priorities of both partners, who are grateful to have a respite from emotional challenges. Good communication between the partners will ensure that neither partner is feeling held back or disconnected from the other. And that brings us to one of the most important of all the spiritual laws in this book: communication.

The Fourth Spiritual Law: Communication

*Honest, non-blaming communication is necessary
on a regular basis in a spiritual relationship.*

The essence of communication is listening. First we must listen to our own thoughts and feelings and take responsibility for them before we can express them to others. Then, once we have expressed how we think and feel in a non-blaming way to others, we need to listen to how others think and feel. At least two thirds of all helpful communication involves listening.

There are two ways to listen. One is with judgment; the other is without judgment. When we listen with judgment, we don't really hear. It doesn't matter whether we are listening to another person or to ourselves. In either case, judgment prevents us from hearing what is being thought or felt.

For example, if I feel angry and I label my anger as bad, I can't let that anger in. I can't experience it or see what might be behind it. By judging my anger, I push it away. I try to dismiss it or perhaps I project it onto you. That doesn't help me acknowledge my anger or find its cause within myself.

Only when we accept the content of what we think or feel or what others think and feel can we really hear what is being said. Without acceptance, listening doesn't happen.

When we interpret what people say, we can't hear them. To hear them, we must accept what they say at face value. This is what they think and feel. We have to assume that they are being honest with us. If we question their honesty, we can't hear them. If we are running judgments about them, we can't hear them. We hear people only when are hearts are open to them.

"Well, people don't always tell the truth," you say. "Am I supposed to keep my heart open to people who are lying to me?"

There is no "supposed to" here. If the person is lying to you, s/he is not communicating. If you are judging him or her, you are not communicating.

Either there is communication or there is not. Heartfelt communication requires honesty on the part of the speaker and acceptance on the part of the listener. When the speaker is blaming and the listener is judging, you don't have communication; you have attack.

To communicate effectively you must do the following:

1. Listen to your thoughts and feelings until you know what they are and understand that they belong only to you.

2. Honestly express how you think and feel to others without blaming them or trying to make them responsible for what you are thinking or how you are feeling.

3. Listen without judgment to any thoughts and feelings others want to convey to you. Remember, what they say, think and feel describes their state of consciousness. It may or may not have anything to do with your own.

If you find that you need to fix other people or defend yourself when other people express their thoughts and feelings to you, you probably aren't listening and it is very likely that your buttons are being pushed. They may be mirroring some part of you which you may not want to look at (see Spiritual Law #5).

The goal of communication is not to improve or to fix anyone. It is simply to tell the truth and hear the truth. Once you have spoken honestly and your partner has heard what you have to say, and vice versa, there will be greater understanding between you. Understanding helps to restore trust and connection. It is a step toward peace.

Before the truth is told without blame and heard without judgment, there is separation between people. The longer people avoid communicating, the deeper the separation and distrust can become. Communication is a bridge over that separation. Once that bridge is established, it may take a while for people to cross over it. But at least the option is there. Reconciliation is a present possibility. Building the bridge is a major step toward peace and communion.

There is one injunction you should heed to increase your likelihood for communicating successfully. Do not attempt to talk with your partner when you are upset or angry. Ask for time out. Tell your partner you will be happy to talk when you figure out how you are feeling. Say "If I talk now, I know I'll say something I don't really mean, and I don't want to do that. I'm going to take a walk. When I'm ready to talk, I'll let you know."

It is important to keep silent until you can own everything that you are thinking and feeling. Otherwise, you will blame your partner for how you feel, and blaming will deepen any misunderstanding or feelings of separation between you. When you are upset, don't strike out at your partner. Take responsibility for your own thoughts and feelings. Take the time to listen to yourself before you try to talk with your partner.

This does not mean that you should stuff your feelings and not speak up. Quite the contrary. If you pretend that everything is okay when you are really angry, you will not be communicating honestly with your partner, nor will you be standing up for yourself. If you feel angry or hurt, it is important that your partner know this. But if you tell him or her in a blaming or attacking way, your communication probably will not be heard. That's why you take the time to own your thoughts and feelings before expressing them.

Good communication always avoids the extremes between attacking someone in an angry way and stuffing the anger. Neither sadism nor masochism contributes to peace or understanding.

Communicating in a non-blaming way is an art that every couple must learn if they want their relationship to grow and thrive. To ensure regular communication, couples should set aside a time each day for connecting honestly with each other.

When you get up in the morning or before you go to bed each night, take ten minutes to share what you are thinking and feeling while your partner listens to you without judgment. Then listen without interrupting while your partner shares what s/he is thinking and feeling with you. This daily ritual helps to establish a culture of communication that you can rely on when you and/or your partner are upset and really need to talk in an honest, non-blaming way.

Good communication helps you and your partner stay emotionally connected. The more you are able to listen to each other without judgment, the more you will come to know and respect each other as separate people. You will be able to honor your partner's experience even when it is different from your own. And you will know that, as much as you care about your partner, you are not responsible for how s/he thinks or feels in any moment. You don't have to fix your partner's pain or make your partner's sadness go away. All you need to do is accept what your partner's experience is and hold it in a compassionate way.

When you and your partner are not trying to fix, improve or redeem each other, you don't become enmeshed and co-dependent. You can really hear each other and offer one another genuine support. You can empower each other to find strength and guidance within.

When you listen and accept your partner, you come to realize that s/he is perfect just the way s/he is. Whatever s/he is thinking or feeling is okay. You can feel compassion for your partner's pain, struggle or ambivalence, without feeling responsible for it. You can just let it be. You can just listen and accept.

You can be present with your partner just by listening without judgment. You don't have to do anything or say anything in particular. You are fine just the way you are. Your partner is okay the way s/he is. You can rest in the perfection of the moment, even when your partner is upset. By holding the conviction that all is well without trying to fix anyone, you don't reinforce your partner's negative emotions, but instead offer her an opportunity to accept her experience and take responsibility for her happiness right here and now.

Your partner can do the same for you by listening to you without judgment when you are upset. You can make it much easier for your partner to do this if you can get in touch with why you are upset before you attempt to talk. Once you have some insight into what your upset is all about, then you can take responsibility for it. You can let your partner know how you are feeling without making him/her responsible for it. You can say "I got triggered by what you said or did" and then go on to talk about what is happening for you.

You make "I" statements, not "You" statements. You don't say "You made me angry," because that statement is false. Nobody can make you angry. Your anger is and will always be your responsibility; you can't give it to anyone else.

Here's an example of how someone can learn to take responsibility for what he is feeling and communicate it in a non-blaming way:

Telling the Truth in a Non-Blaming Way: An Example

John thinks Marsha is pushy and rude. That's his judgment and he is responsible for it.

If John looks deeply enough at his judgment of Marsha, he might see that she pushes his Mommy buttons. John's mother was pushy too. John often feels that people don't give him enough space, but he doesn't usually ask for space in a direct way. For example, instead of telling Marsha what is coming up for him, he says something to her in a sarcastic, passive-aggressive way. That triggers Marsha's anger.

Once Marsha gets angry, John wants to go and hide. That's his pattern. Instead of standing up for himself and saying what he needs, John withdraws and attacks in a clandestine way.

If John keeps looking at his own motives, he will see how Marsha is mirroring him. He has a problem expressing his anger, so he triggers anger in some-one else. Then, he has to face the anger.

If John could have owned his discomfort with Marsha and expressed it directly, he might have avoided some of this misunderstanding. He might have said "Marsha I want to own that I have some judgments coming up about you. I experience you as pushy and I get edgy when you are around. I think that's why I find myself being sarcastic with you. Now, I know this is my issue. The same thing happened with my mother. I didn't feel I could be myself around her, so I just withdrew and attacked from a distance. I know I'm doing that with you and I don't want to keep doing this. I want to be able to get to know you and let you in. I just want you to know that it's hard for me."

By communicating his discomfort directly to Marsha, John lets her know that <u>he</u> has a problem and she is just triggering it. She isn't responsible for his problem. It's <u>his</u> responsibility and <u>he's</u> trying to deal with it.

Marsha now has more information about what is going on for John. She can be more sensitive to where he's at. Maybe next time she goes into John's office she *will knock first. Or, if she forgets to knock, and John says something to her in a sarcastic way, she will be able to overlook it and know that it's John's issue.*

When the truth is expressed in a non-blaming way, people can retain appropriate boundaries with one another and overlook small trespasses or indiscretions. They don't engage on an unconscious level, where the deeper wounds of the psyche can be mutually triggered.

In my book *Living in the Heart: The Affinity Process and the Path of Unconditional Love and Acceptance*, I discuss at length how people can listen to each other without judgment and tell the truth to one another in a non-blaming way. The fourteen guidelines for sharing in the *Affinity Process* can be used by couples to communicate responsibly and effectively.

These skills are not learned overnight. They require constant practice. We aren't taught in school how to take responsibility for our own experience or how to respect the experience of others. Yet these skills are essential if we are going to experience peace within our hearts and minds, and peace with other people.

The Fifth Spiritual Law: Mirroring

What we don't like about our partner
reflects back to us what we don't like
and can't accept about ourselves.

If we are trying to run away from ourselves, the last place we want to try and hide is in a relationship. The purpose of an intimate relationship is to help us learn to face our own fears, judgments, doubts and insecurities. While we may be successful in hiding our dark side from our conscious awareness while living alone, it is almost impossible to do so in an intimate relationship. Moreover, there is absolutely no chance we can hide our doubts and fears when we decide to live with someone.

Living with someone is like being in a pressure cooker. There's no cooking el dente, no slow sauteing here. We're going to get cooked all the way through whether we like it or not

After beginning a relationship, it usually isn't long before our doubts and fears come up about the other person. We're not sure we're with the right partner. S/he's short with us, even rude at times.

79

S/he doesn't tell us that s/he loves us as often as we'd like to hear it. We go on finding fault with the other person, wondering if s/he really wants to be with us. We don't take the time to check it out with our partner. To do that, would mean reality-testing, and we prefer to have our own opinion. We'd rather see the problem in our partner than in ourselves.

When our fears and doubts are triggered by our partner, as they will be in any intimate relationship, we don't want to face them directly. We don't say "Oh, here is my insecurity coming up for me to look at." We blame our partner for how and what we're feeling: "I'm feeling insecure because s/he didn't speak kindly to me."

But what if the insecurity is already there and our partner just happened to trigger it. Perhaps Dad spoke harshly to us and, as we grew up, we felt that we weren't good enough. Even though Dad may not speak to us that way now, we may be carrying around that old hurt subconsciously. We would not know we still had that wound if someone didn't trigger our awareness of it.

So our partner says something to us in an off-hand, joking way and it cuts right to the bone. And the next thing we know we are feeling really hurt and violated. Our partner did not intend to be hurtful to us. S/he was perhaps a bit careless or even sarcastic, but s/he didn't know we would react the way we did.

We can focus on our partner's action, find fault with that and try to get our partner to speak more kindly to us in the future, or we can take responsibility for the deep pain and feelings of rejection that are welling up for us right now. In the first case, we refuse to deal with our pain by making someone else responsible for it. In the second case, we let that pain in, own it, and then let our partner know what is going on for us.

What's most important about this interaction is not "You were rude to me" but "What you said triggered my feelings that I am not good enough." That's what I need to look at. When people aren't being nice to me, I think that they don't like me, that something is wrong with me, that I'm not good enough. That internal dynamic belongs to me, not to my partner. My partner just triggers the old tape "I'm not good enough." I've been carrying that tape around since I was two years old.

Do I want to change my partner's behavior or do I want to change the tape? Trying to change my partner probably won't work very well but, even if it did, someone else (my sister, for example) might come along and push the buttons on the tape recorder. There are plenty of people who, unbeknownst to them, are quite adept at pushing my buttons. I can't change them all.

So why focus on the trigger when I can remove the bullets? When the gun isn't loaded, nobody gets hurt, even if the trigger is pulled.

The question I must ask is not "Who's attacking me?" but "Why do I feel attacked?" Or, to use the above example "Why do I feel not good enough?"

Maybe I feel "not good enough" because Daddy did not give me the approval I wanted from him and I keep on looking in vain for that approval from other men. I do this in a couple of different ways. Sometimes I choose a partner who, like Daddy, is very critical of me, so that I can become conscious of my Daddy wound. Other times I choose someone who is very different from Daddy, but as soon as that person is displeased with me, I still feel I am not good enough. In either case, my

Daddy wound gives me an antenna for criticism. I can spot it a thousand miles away.

If I want to heal my Daddy wound, I have to realize that there are going to be many times when I want someone to be nice to me and approve of me and that person is going to be cool, or rude, or mean, or critical. And that doesn't mean that I'm not good enough. That means the person isn't able to meet my needs right now. That's all. It's not a reflection on me. It might not be anything other than a temporary reflection on that human being, who might be feeling stressed out or impatient.

I am responsible for healing my Daddy wound, even though you may be the one who triggered it. When I accept this responsibility, I try not to blame you when you push my buttons. I say: "This is about me. When I think that you are being mean to me, I think that you don't like me and you don't want to be with me. I start to feel like I'm not good enough. I'm not worthy of love. That's what comes up for me. It's not true, but I think it's true."

We all have our private storehouse of illusions — beliefs about ourselves or others that aren't true. When we challenge those illusions, they dissolve, because only the truth can stand our scrutiny.

Every time we are triggered by our partner, we have the opportunity to see through our illusions and drop them once and for all. It doesn't take all that much insight to see that the belief "When others aren't nice to me it means that I'm not good enough" is false. But I must be clear what my belief is if I am going to challenge it.

An intimate relationship gives you and your partner endless opportunities to look into your core beliefs about yourselves. Your partner is the cattle prod moving you toward the most sensitive areas of self-delusion. S/he helps you wake up by bringing old wounds and false beliefs up into your conscious attention. When you have a fight with your partner, it has little to do with the specifics of the situation and a lot to do with the inner demons which are disturbed and brought out into the light of day.

Your partner is not responsible for your demons, nor are you responsible for his or hers. But you are midwives to each other's growth into conscious awareness. Living with a partner is like living with parents or children. All these relationships push our deepest buttons. They trigger us, set off inner and outer explosions, so that our fears can no longer stay hidden. It isn't always pleasant business.

If we expect it to be pleasant all or even most of the time, then we will be sadly disappointed. Every relationship moves from romance to realism to the depths of despair. Couples fall from grace just as individuals do. Each has a dark night of the soul, a grappling with the demonic realm. The couples who face their demons and walk through their fears have won a decisive battle against ignorance. They hit existential bottom and realize that the only reason they are together is to learn how to love and accept themselves. That is the path to Ascension.

It is a spiritual law that whatever bothers us about someone else shows us a part of ourselves we are unwilling to love and accept. Blaming or finding fault with our partners does not help us meet that part of ourselves or redeem it. Yet that is the sacred purpose of relationship.

Our partners are the mirrors that help us come face to face with ourselves. Whatever way we have trouble loving or accepting ourselves will be reflected back to us by our partner. Sometimes the reflection is a direct one and sometimes it is indirect. For example, if we experience our partner as selfish, it might be because we ourselves are acting selfishly. Or it might be because our partner stands up for himself and that is what we have been unwilling to do for ourselves.

We can be angry at our partners, but this is pure self-deception. It disguises the anger we feel at ourselves. And that anger is what we must ultimately come to terms with. After all, it is not our partner's mistakes that haunt us, but our own. We are responsible for our mistakes and we know it. Forgiving those mistakes is sometimes very difficult for us. We have to learn to be gentle with ourselves. We have to realize that our mistakes don't condemn us. They just provide us with an opportunity to grow and to learn.

We may try to blame our partners, but the one we really blame is ourselves. We are the one who ultimately gets crucified or gets off the cross and walks free. Let's remember that the next time we find fault with our partners.

Every relationship is a mirror in which we learn to see and embrace all that we are: the parts of self that we like and admire and the parts that we judge and detest. When we get angry at or upset with our partner, we are externalizing the anger that we feel toward ourselves. Our partner becomes a target for the projection of our self-hatred.

No one wants to be a target for someone else's rage. Yet many relationships shipwreck in the high seas of mutual projection. This is a sad, but not uncommon fact.

The only way to avoid the destruction of the relationship is to take direct responsibility for the thoughts and feelings that arise from the depths of our psyche and hold our partner harmless. "I know this is about me, not about my partner," we must continually say to ourselves whenever we are triggered. When we can own our own internal struggle and refrain from projecting the responsibility for our pain onto our partner, our partner becomes our greatest teacher.

When such in-depth learning about ourselves is mutual in our relationship, our partnership is transformed into a spiritual pathway for self-knowledge and fulfillment. We learn from our partner what no one else could teach us. How many people are skillful at both pushing our buttons and holding us compassionately as we encounter the depth of our own self-hatred. There is no better guru on the planet than our partner when we have embraced the spiritual purpose of our relationship.

Our relationship journey comes full circle when we can see and embrace both our partner's innocence and our own. When we have moved through the shadowy world of mutual attack and projection out into the light of mutual acceptance and forgiveness, we are given custody of the Holy Grail itself, the ultimate symbol of psychic integration, power and wholeness.

The rewards for the journey are profound, indeed unspeakable. But few of us dare to travel the whole route from fragmentation to wholeness. Few of us have the courage to fall from grace, bury our impotent fantasies of romance, and experience the shadowy world of our demons in order to learn to take responsibility for our own healing. Our partner opens the door for us, but s/he can't walk through it in our place.

Many of us teeter-totter on the edge of responsibility only to turn away when the relationship becomes painful. We don't like looking in the mirror.

Again and again, we buy into our own romantic fantasies, which are nothing more than an escape from self, thinking we will find the perfect mate around the next corner.

Every relationship not dedicated to mutual growth and self-revelation ends at these fiery gates. Only the most courageous souls — those who have taken the time to walk through their own fear and pain — pass through. Their relationships have become classrooms for experiential learning, laboratories in which they patiently study and build the spiritual vehicle that will ultimately bring them home.

The Sixth Spiritual Law: Taking Responsibility

In a spiritual relationship, each partner takes responsibility for his or her thoughts, feelings and experiences.

It is ironic perhaps that relationship, with its apparent emphasis on sharing and companionship, asks us only to take responsibility for ourselves. What we think, feel, and experience belongs to us. And what our partner thinks, feels, and experiences belongs to him or her. We are never responsible for our partner's experience and our partner is never responsible for ours. The beauty of this spiritual law is lost on those who need to make their partners responsible for their happiness or their pain.

Though we move from an "I" context into a "We" context in relationship, we don't lose the spiritual purity of the "I". I still can decide only for myself and you for yourself. I cannot decide for you nor can you decide for me. That essential responsibility does not go away when we enter a relationship.

Unfortunately, many of us forget our responsibility to ourselves as soon as we enter a relationship. We want to make our partners responsible for our happiness and, when they push our buttons, we want to make them responsible for our pain. Our partners do the same thing to us. In the game of co-dependent love, boundaries quickly fade and we stop taking responsibility for our own thoughts, feelings, and experiences. Nothing derails a relationship faster than these excursions into guilt and blame.

We forget the discipline we must bring to our own lives. We are not always happy. When we live alone, we have many moments of sadness, self-judgment, and feelings of unworthiness or failure. We need to ride out these moments and hold these thoughts and feelings compassionately or we cannot function in life. What makes us think that we won't carry these emotional lows into our relationship? Moreover, what makes us think that we won't have to be just as compassionate with ourselves in a relationship as we need to be when we are living alone?

The truth is, we need to be <u>more</u> compassionate with ourselves when we live with someone else. We need to be <u>more</u> responsible for our thoughts, feelings, and actions. This is the case because our egoic tendency is to blame our partner for our unhappiness, even when we realize intellectually that s/he isn't responsible for our experience.

When we live alone, we blame ourselves. When we live with someone else, we blame our partner. Blaming our partner is an act of projection. Rather than look directly at our own fears and insecurities, we make our partner responsible for how miserable we feel.

To refrain from projection is one of the greatest challenges of relationship. To own what belongs to us — our thoughts, feelings, and actions — and disown what belongs to our partner — his or her thoughts, feelings, and actions — helps us to establish healthy boundaries with our partner. Then, when we understand where our responsibility is and isn't, we still need to hold our own experience and that of our partner compassionately.

You are not here to fix or redeem your partner and s/he is not here to fix or redeem you. You aren't here to make judgments of one another or to make each other responsible for your personal sadness, pain or unhappiness. You are here to accept, embrace, and take responsibility for your entire experience, regardless of what it is and to support your partner in doing the same.

When your partner is sad or angry, you need to know that those feelings are his/her responsibility, not yours. You may have triggered the feelings, but you are not their ultimate cause, nor are you responsible for changing how your partner feels. Knowing that you are not responsible for what s/he is feeling doesn't mean that you cease to care. You can care, deeply in fact, without taking on a responsibility that does not belong to you.

Oftentimes, your partner doesn't even want you to try to fix or change what s/he is feeling. S/he just wants you to listen and understand what s/he is experiencing. You can do this without taking on responsibility. Indeed, if you try to take responsibility when it does not belong to you, you will increase your emotional burden and compromise your ability to support your partner in an unconditionally loving way.

Eschewing false responsibility enables you to respond in a caring way. You don't feel threatened by your partner's pain or sadness. You know it's not your fault and it's not your job to fix it. So you can listen with compassion. You can send your partner simple, heart-felt blessings.

On the other side of the coin, your emotional lows are your responsibility. "This belongs to me, not to my partner," you need to keep saying when your judgments about your partner come up or when you are feeling emotionally distraught. If you project your pain onto your partner, you will be pushing him or her away. That won't get you the sympathy or the acknowledgement that you want. It will just create greater separation.

The challenge is to tell the truth about how you are feeling (eg. I'm feeling sad) without trying to make your partner responsible for what you are feeling (eg. I'm sad because you weren't home on time). That means taking the time to feel your sadness and learn from it. Maybe you have some ongoing abandonment issues that are triggered when someone you love isn't there for you. Your partner may unwittingly trigger these issues, but s/he is not responsible for them. If you take the time to experience your own feelings, instead of projecting them, you will be able to tell your partner how you feel in a non-blaming way. "I had a lot of sadness coming up when I got home tonight and saw that you weren't there. I had really been looking forward to seeing you and I felt disappointed. I wondered if you really cared about me. And then I got into thinking of all the times I have cared about people and they haven't been there for me, starting with my mother, and then my first wife. I really got into it. I cried for fifteen minutes."

This tells your partner exactly where you are at emotionally without blaming him or her for what you are experiencing. Because you don't blame, you give your partner the opportunity to connect in a genuine way with how you are feeling. S/he can feel your sadness and your pain without feeling that s/he is in any way responsible for them.

Lest you think that learning to communicate in this responsible way is easy, let me reassure you that it is not. We are not taught how to do this. Indeed, learning to take responsibility for our experience goes against most of what we have been taught. It requires great courage and willingness to learn on our part.

Most of us are so busy looking outward for our partner's support and approval that we don't take the time to look within our own hearts and minds.

If we want to take responsibility for our experience, we need to stop looking outside and start looking within.

As soon as we do, we see how merciless we are with ourselves. We are constantly judging how we think and what we feel. We don't like the way life shows up and we resist it or push it away. We develop an antagonistic relationship with our own thoughts, feelings and experiences. We don't accept our life. We don't embrace our experience as it unfolds.

To become responsible for our own experience we must accept it as it is. We need to drop our interpretations and our judgments about it, or at least be aware of them. Our experience is what it is. Whatever is happening for us — laughter, tears, joy, sadness, judgment, regret — is acceptable and we can own it. We don't need to make our partner responsible for how we think or feel.

Accepting our life as it is and taking responsibility for what we think, feel and do enables us to experience our own creative power. We can dream, take risks, be ourselves. We can make mistakes. We can learn and grow. The whole process is liberating, as long as we know how to be gentle with ourselves.

However, if we need to be perfect, if we need to measure up to our own rigid expectations or those of our partner, we won't be able to experience the fullness of who we are. We will limit ourselves. We will force ourselves to live inside a box.

If we do that, we are responsible. No one else is to blame. Maybe Mommy or Daddy intimidated us with their perfectionism, but they aren't there any more. We have internalized their perfectionism. We are our own judge and jury. We hold ourselves hostage.

When we know we are responsible for what happens, we are free to make a different choice. That may not be easy to do — we have years of conditioning to undo — but it is not impossible. In fact, when we take responsibility for our own lives here and now, it is amazing what we can accomplish. When we were blaming others for our problems, all our energy went into confirming the problem. Now, by letting others off the hook, we can begin moving forward toward the result that we want. Now, we are challenged to have our own vision. We lay down Mommy's and Daddy's vision of us and we start all over again. We find out who we are. We move toward our own joy and creative freedom. We make our own mistakes and we forgive ourselves. We enter the path to self-realization.

When we are in relationship, it isn't easy to empower ourselves, especially if we are still angry at our parents. More often than not, our partner makes a good stand-in for Mommy or Daddy, and we continue to play out our dramas of shame and blame. To grow, we not only need to let our parents off the hook; we need to take our partner off the hook too.

If we don't choose to move toward our joy, it isn't our partner's fault. The choices that we make — even the choice to deny ourselves or sacrifice for our partner — are our responsibility. Just because our partner is willing to accept our sacrifice doesn't make him or her responsible for it. Who is the one who offered to sacrifice or acquiesced to our partner's demand?

Many of us are afraid to take responsibility for our lives because we equate responsibility with blame. We think "I screwed up; it's my fault." We think making a mistake condemns us, so we'd rather give the responsibility to someone else. We don't want to face our errors. In our minds, owning our mistakes is tantamount to confessing our guilt and inviting punishment.

Being punished for our mistakes may be an Old Testament concept, but we give it a contemporary resting place. "An eye for an eye, a tooth for a tooth" lives not just in the collective unconscious, but in our own personal storehouse of fear and guilt. Our parents introduced us to the concept, and we introduced our children to it. The blood line runs deep.

Can we find self-forgiveness in the midst of our merciless judgment of ourselves? If we can, finding it will entail bringing a different attitude toward our mistakes. If we make a mistake, it does not mean that we are bad and need to be punished. It means that we need to learn something. We were moving off course and can now find correction. It is a positive event, not a negative one.

Seeing our mistakes as opportunities for learning and correction removes the scourge of perfectionism from our consciousness. When we are able to be gentle with and forgiving of our own mistakes, it is easier to feel compassionate toward others when they make mistakes and ask for our understanding. Having learned to forgive ourselves, we cannot withhold forgiveness from others. Having been forgiven, we cannot withhold forgiveness from ourselves.

The dialog of forgiveness is a far cry from the reactive litany of mutual blame. But to come into this dialog each person must be willing to take responsibility for his or her experience and respect the experience of other people.

That means that you can no longer make your partner responsible for what you think, feel, or do and your partner can no longer make you responsible for what s/he thinks, feels or does. S/he must accept your experience as it is and you must accept his or hers. That is one of the greatest gifts you can give each another.

Now, when you communicate, you let each other in to what you are thinking and feeling, but you don't try to tell each other what to do. You don't offer advice or ask for approval. You listen to each other without judgment and support each other in finding the answer within your own hearts.

The "We" consciousness in your relationship is born of the strength and integrity of the "I" consciousness or it is a sham. When you and your partner are honest with each other and responsible for your own experiences, the "We" has profound meaning. When honesty or responsibility is lacking, the "We" can only be a betrayal of self.

You can be sure that God did not create relationship so that we would betray ourselves. Indeed, it is quite the opposite. The purpose of relationship is to insure that we learn to be faithful to ourselves.

One of the paradoxes of relationship as a spiritual path is that we give our power away to others in order to learn to honor ourselves more completely. We become co-dependent with others in order to learn how to have better boundaries. We blame others so that we can learn to be gentle with ourselves and forgive our own mistakes.

It is all a set-up. We look for love and happiness through other people only to learn that we can find love and happiness only in our own hearts and minds. That is the recognition in which the "We" is born. It is a psycho-spiritual event of great importance and intensity. It creates the spiritual body or vehicle of partnership through which both people will grow to actualize their unique potential. It is the promise of relationship fulfilled, the creative synergy that results from the coming together of two awakened and responsible human beings.

The Seventh Spiritual Law: Forgiveness

In a spiritual relationship, forgiveness of ourselves and our partner is a moment-to-moment practice.

As we attempt to embody in our consciousness and relationships the spiritual laws discussed in this book, we need to remember that we aren't going to do it perfectly. There is no perfection when it comes to human experience.

You will make mistakes as you endeavor to follow the teachings in this book and so will your partner. You are both human. That means that together you reach to the heights of heaven and the depths of hell. Angels and devils live in your embrace and move with you in your perpetual journey toward self-forgiveness.

If you expect your relationship to be only happy and inspiring, how will you deal with the times when you feel repelled and disconnected from your partner? How will you deal with your sadness, your doubts and fears when they come up?

No relationship, no matter how well suited the partners are to one another, no matter how much they love each other, is going to be free of struggle and turmoil. In any relationship, there are inevitable ups and downs, moments of connection and disconnection.

How we hold the moments of disconnection is as important as how we celebrate the moments of connection. Can we hold our own pain and our partner's pain compassionately or do we deny it and try to make it go away?

When we are triggered by our partner, do we endeavor to find the source of our anger or hurt inside ourselves, or do we insist that we wouldn't feel this way if our partner treated us differently? Do we use the challenges of the relationship to look more deeply within ourselves and embrace the parts of ourselves we do not like, or do we run away and hide or threaten to leave the relationship every time there are misunderstandings?

Do we rebound well from our arguments with our partners and find a way to reconnect? Or do we hold onto our feelings of alienation and begin to shut down our hearts?

All of us tend to run away or to fight when we get scared. To think that we aren't going to get scared is absurd. The question is what is our pattern when we get scared: fight or flight?

If our pattern is to criticize or attack our partner, then our responsibility is to be aware of that pattern and ask ourselves what is happening for us when we are engaged in it: What feelings are we not facing by criticizing or attacking our partner? Is there a part of us that doesn't want to be in this relationship and would rather be left alone? Are we really afraid of intimacy even though we are asking for it?

If our pattern is to run away, we need to be aware of that too and ask: "What are we running away from that we don't want to face in ourselves? Is it our neediness, our desire for external validation which we continue to seek even when people are critical of us? Are we avoiding intimacy by choosing partners who cannot meet our needs? And, if so, what are these people teaching us? Is it possible that we need to learn to give ourselves the validation we are seeking from our partners?

Our fears bring up our deeper emotional issues, whatever they are. Every single one of us has those issues and they are bound to come up in the pressure cooker of relationship.

Every couple must ask themselves "Are we willing to deal with our fears when they come up? Can we create a safe space together in which this material can be held gently and compassionately?"

Creating that sacred space is essential for the long term success of any relationship. If partners cannot create a shared safe space together, how can they rebound from fights and misunderstandings?

Each person must feel comfortable going to the other and telling the truth in a non-blaming way about how s/he thinks and feels in that moment. Once that communication is heard, it can be held gently by both people. This is the way that bridges of forgiveness are built.

Asking for forgiveness does not mean going to the other person and saying "I'm sorry." It means going to the other person and saying "This is what's happening for me. I hope that you can accept it and work with it. I'm doing the best I can." It's learning to accept our own situation, even when it is difficult, and offering our partner an opportunity to accept it, even though that might not be easy for him or her. Our acceptance of what's happening for us when we want to judge it is self-forgiveness. Our acceptance of our partner's situation when we want to judge it or find fault with it is the extension of our self-forgiveness to him or her. It says to our partner "I forgive myself for judging you. My goal is to accept you just the way you are."

Saying "I'm sorry" to our partner may help us to forgive ourselves or it may not. If our partner withholds the words of forgiveness that we seek, we may find that asking outwardly for forgiveness doesn't work very well. In the end, we must be willing to forgive ourselves. And that is an internal proposition.

Until we forgive ourselves, we cannot meet our partner on fresh ground. We continue to feel guilt or resentment. Resentment toward the other is simply disguised self-hatred. Guilt is merely internalized anger. Both are attacks on ourselves.

When we realize that there is only one person to forgive in any situation and that is ourselves, we finally understand that we have been given the keys to the kingdom. By forgiving ourselves for what we think or feel about others, we can be free to respond to them in a different way the next time we see them. We don't have to hold onto the past.

A relationship is easily crippled by its own past

baggage. When anger and hurt are carried around, there is an undercurrent of judgment and irritation that surfaces when new challenges arise. Fueled by mutual resentment, little problems that normally could be resolved now become major issues. The air needs to be cleared. The burden of past misunderstandings needs to be laid to rest.

It is impossible to find forgiveness as long as we are blaming ourselves or the other person. We must find ways to move from blame to responsibility. When we own our thoughts and feelings and our partners do the same, we can see how our behavior mutually affects one another. We don't have to condemn our behavior or our partner's. We can simply see the mechanics of it: how we push each other's buttons and react to one another. When we are reactive, neither one of us is to blame, but both of us are responsible.

We are responsible for what we create together. If we are both in pain, we are both responsible for it. Perhaps we don't understand the unconscious factors that contribute to our pain and mutual reactivity, but this does not make us any less responsible. Our challenge and our responsibility is

107

to become conscious of our own unconscious wounds so that we can understand how we contribute to the overall discomfort and dysfunction of the situation.

Forgiveness does not mean anything without awareness of our issues and willingness to move toward correction. Pain is a wake up call. It urges us to become aware and responsible. There are a number of strategies for becoming responsible for our contribution to the difficulties in our relationship. We can seek counseling, take a personal growth or inner child workshop, do breath work or body centered therapy, or become involved in a therapy group for couples.

Many people seek help in their relationships only when mutual trust has been destroyed and it is too late to put the pieces back together. Don't wait until your relationship falls apart to seek help. Recognize when you and your partner are having difficulty rebounding from your mutual trespasses. Notice when resentments are being carried around and are fueling new conflicts. If you see that you and your partner are losing your emotional resilience and are starting to blame each other more for the problems that arise, this is the time to ask for help. There is nothing weak or cowardly in asking for help when it is needed. On the contrary, it is a gesture of mutual courage, strength and caring about your relationship.

Another way to address the issue of mutual trespass is for both couples to keep a running log of how they are feeling in relationship to one another. When anger comes up for one person and the other person feels attacked, both people take a break and go write in their journal or log. While journaling, the person who felt anger tries to take responsibility for his anger and discover the fear behind it, and the person who felt attacked describes how s/he feels and explores whether her pattern is to run away, get angry back or to stuff the anger.

At the end of the day, when they are feeling receptive to one another, the couple takes fifteen or twenty minutes to share part or all of their journal entries with one another. While one person is sharing, the other does not respond or defend himself, but just listens in silence and practices acceptance. "This is my partner's experience," he keeps saying internally. "It doesn't matter what I think or feel about it. I just need to listen to what her experience is so that I can understand it. I don't have to do anything about it. I don't have to try to fix anything here." Then, when that person is finished sharing, the other person shares while his partner listens without responding.

If this ritual is performed on a daily basis it will help the couple develop a profound awareness of each other's thoughts and feelings. Awareness of trespass naturally leads to correction when there is no blame involved. The couple will simply start to be more aware of the impact their words and actions have on each other. It's not that they try to change their behavior toward one another so much as it is that their awareness spontaneously and effortlessly leads to modifications in offensive behavior.

This exercise can be used in conjunction with therapy or, if it works, in lieu of it. For those who can't afford the cost of counseling, this daily ritual can be an affordable alternative. It should be clear, however, that the ritual is only as powerful as the mutual commitment of the partners enables it to be.

Many people think that forgiveness has to be hard work. They think that it requires us to change ourselves or to ask our partners to change. While change does come as a result of the practice of for-giveness, it cannot be demanded. When you feel that you must change to save your relationship, you may resist or capitulate in guilt. Either reaction will pre-vent authentic change from occurring.

When we take away blame, awareness can work miracles. Just knowing what our partner thinks and feels and accepting it (without feeling responsible for causing it or needing to fix it) creates greater sensitivity toward our partner. Our thoughts, words and actions will then embody that sensitivity and our partner will feel the difference in how we are responding to him or her.

This is a gradual process, consisting of many small steps and many little changes. Correction occurs slowly and naturally. It is not forced. The more we listen to our partner and accept his experi-ence, the more sensitive and responsive to him we become. After a month or two of practicing this sim-ple ritual, the quality of communication in the relationship will be transformed.

Forgiveness does not require outer change so much as it does inner change. When we stop blam-ing our partner and begin taking responsibility for our own pain and discontent, the process of forgiveness starts to work. Ultimately, we stop being so hard on ourselves. We learn to accept our mistakes and learn from them. We stop pounding the nails of self-judgment into our own hands and feet.

Forgiveness is not a doing so much as it is an undoing. It enables us to undo blame and guilt. It enables us to forgive ourselves for attacking our partner and forgive our partner for attacking us. It wipes the slate clean of resentment. It enables us to start fresh with our partners. We don't have to keep carrying the trauma of the past around with us. We don't have to keep reminding our partner of what s/he said or did yesterday or last week.

Only an ongoing forgiveness process enables us to stay present in our partnerships as they move through their inevitable ups and downs. Forgiveness wipes the slate clean of shame and blame and enables us to reconnect emotionally to our partner and recommit to our relationship.

part three

changing the form
of a relationship

Transformation

The only thing that is changeless is change itself. No relationship lasts forever. Even couples who have lived together for most of their lives are separated when one of them dies. Other relationships run their course after two or three years. Every relationship has a beginning, a middle, and an end. No relationship lasts forever.

When two people can no longer grow together, it is time for them to re-evaluate their commitment to one another and consider changing the form of their relationship. For example, a couple who has been living together with difficulty might decide to live apart and continue to see each other as lovers, or they might decide to separate completely.

There is no right or wrong here. It's up to you and your partner how you want to revise your commitment to one another. It's always best when the two of you can agree on the new form you want your relationship to take. But when agreement is not possible, it is wise to choose the form desired by the person who is in the most pain. Time and space away from the relationship may enable emotional healing to take place and generate greater clarity about the relationship. Then, the nature of the commitment can be re-negotiated.

It is important that separation take place with dignity and with love. Even when a relationship does not work, both people have still shared and learned a lot together. There should be mutual gratitude for the good times, as well as for the challenging times when greater insight and understanding was gained.

Before you and your partner decide to terminate your relationship, ask yourself if you have learned all that the relationship can teach you? If not, can you change the form of the relationship in such a way as to make learning easier for both of you?

Try not to leave the relationship or make decisions about it in anger. Calm down and ask your partner to make time for a heart-to-heart talk. Tell the truth about what's happening for you and ask your partner to do the same. Don't leave out anything that's important. Just listen to each other. Don't feel that you have to make an immediate decision.

Take the time to really be with your feelings and really digest what your partner confides to you. If you find it helpful, take some time alone away from your partner to get clear. Then come back together and share again. See if you have some areas of agreement with your partner on which both of you can act.

Let your coming apart (or transformation in the form of your relationship) take as long as it needs to. It is a process, after all, just as putting your lives together was a process. If you take the time to separate with mutual understanding and forgiveness, you will have a far easier time coming to completion.

You do yourself and your partner a disservice if you don't take this time to support each other as you make the transition from one form of relationship to another. It is the only loving thing to do. Moreover, it will make it far easier for both of you to move on without a bitter taste in your mouth.

Detachment

Once you have reached an agreement and taken the time to support each other in making the transition to the new form of your relationship, it is time to detach from the old form. Say, for example, you and your partner decide that you want to continue as friends, but don't want to be sexual. When you are in transition, you may make love once or twice or you may lie in bed together holding each other. Doing that helps both of you feel supported. However, there will be a point when sleeping together is no longer helpful or appropriate. It holds you back from moving in the direction you have chosen. At this time, good boundaries are necessary. It is time to detach.

Part of the process of detachment is grieving the old form of the relationship. You may shed tears. Your body may still yearn for the other person's touch. You may feel other physical or emotional withdrawal symptoms. This is natural and will take as long as it takes. There is no correct period of time for grieving the loss of a relationship or a particular aspect of connection with someone. Accepting your experience and patiently going through it enables you to come to completion.

Don't beat yourself up if it takes you a long time to grieve a relationship that was important to you. You don't have to compare yourself to other people. If friends push you to socialize before you are ready, tell them that you appreciate their concern for you, but you just don't feel ready. Ask them to support you in staying with your own process.

Sometimes we don't really learn the lessons a relationship brings to us until after we break up with a person. While we are in the relationship we may feel too much conflict and pressure to really look at our own issues. Later, when the pressure is off, and we are grieving the connection with the other person, we may be more willing to look at our own issues.

We don't detach fully from our relationship until we begin to learn the issues that our partnership brought up for us. If we try to move on to other relationships before we have dealt with these core issues, we will likely recreate the same lessons with a new partner. That just deepens our woundedness and our sense of futility about ever connecting in an authentic way with a life partner.

Our time out of relationship is just as important as our time in it. Indeed, it may be said that, when we are alone, we are preparing to be in relationship and, when we are in relationship, we are preparing to be alone. Hopefully, we begin to learn the lesson of our last relationship before we go into a new one. Then we can experience new challenges and grow in new ways.

Coming to completion with a relationship is an

internal task, not an interactive one. We do the best we can to separate in a dignified and loving way and to support each other in pursuing our new lives. That makes it easier for us to come to completion. But completion itself depends on our willingness to use the relationship to move into a greater appreciation of and fidelity to who we are and what we need. Then, we don't betray ourselves in the next relationship.

The more clear we get about who we are and what we want in a relationship, the easier it will be for us to be honest with others. That honesty will prevent us from getting involved in relationships with people who are unwilling to respect our experience or to work consciously with the unconscious material that inevitably comes up in a relationship.

Re-Committing to Love

One of the primary goals of any relationship is to learn to love and accept our partner without conditions. Sometimes we are able to do this within the initial form of the relationship. Sometimes we need to change the form of the relationship to be able to do it. But whatever happens, the goal remains the same.

Even if we decide that we must separate from our partner and can never see him or her again, we still have the choice to send this person unconditional love and blessings. Indeed, if we are sending our partner anything less than this, we can be sure that we have not learned the lesson of the relationship.

Relationships that end in shame and blame have a kind of karmic energy around them. Partners who continue to hold resentments toward one another will tend to attract new partners who will help them learn the lessons of the relationship once and for all. It is a fact of life that when we don't learn our lessons in a gentle way, we get a more compelling version of the same curriculum. This doesn't happen to punish us, but to help us learn.

Another one of the primary goals of relationship is to help us deepen in our commitment to love and accept ourselves. Whenever we betray ourselves with our partner, we need to come to terms with our lack of commitment to ourselves. We need to see the way we give our power away in relationship and take responsibility for empowering ourselves. Blaming our partners isn't going to help us do this. If our partner took our power away, it is because we let him or her do it. We are not powerless. We can always walk away from or refuse to cooperate with a situation that does not feel good to us.

The bottom line is that we are responsible for all of the choices that we make. If we enter a relationship that is difficult or painful, we need to find out why. Why are we betraying ourselves? Until we discover the answer to this question, we will continue to ask it in one relationship after another.

This isn't a very gentle way to learn our lessons. Indeed, it is a kind of relentless masochism. It would be better for us to be alone for a while and investigate the causes of our self-betrayal before starting another relationship.

In many cases, forgiveness continues to be an issue long after we have physically separated from our partners. We don't come to completion until we can learn from our mistakes and forgive them, until we can be grateful to our partner for what we learned together.

Every relationship that comes into our lives comes to teach us. We don't always learn the lesson when the relationship brings it. Sometimes we learn weeks, months or even years later. We are not a failure in this respect. We just have a little longer learning curve. As long as we are learning, it doesn't matter how long we are taking.

The major questions we need to ask when we come to the end of our relationship are "Am I holding myself in a loving, compassionate way? Am I forgiving my mistakes and learning from them? Am I holding my partner in a loving and compassionate way? Am I forgiving her mistakes and holding her in the light?"

And if the answer is not "Yes," then let us still aspire to the goal and accept the fact that we have not reached it. Forgiveness happens in its own time. We cannot force it. When we are willing to forgive, forgiveness comes as a gift. If we ask for help in this, our request will not be denied.

May our trespasses against our partner be forgiven, even as we forgive our partner's trespasses against us. Tomorrow is a new day. Let us meet it with hope and confidence, knowing that we are learning, however slowly, the lessons our relationship has asked us to learn.

Namaste

P aul Ferrini is the author of numerous books which help us heal the emotional body and embrace a spirituality grounded in the real challenges of daily life. Paul's work is heart-centered and experiential, empowering us to move through our fear and shame and share who we are authentically with others. Paul Ferrini founded and edited Miracles Magazine, a publication devoted to telling Miracle Stories offering hope and inspiration to all of us. Paul's conferences, retreats and Affinity Group Process have helped thousands of people deepen their practice of forgiveness and open their hearts to the Divine presence in themselves and others. For more information on Paul's workshops and retreats or The Affinity Group Process, contact Heartways Press, P.O. Box 181, South Deerfield, MA 01373 or call 413-665-0555.

New Titles from Heartways Press
by Paul Ferrini

The Relationship Book
You've Been Waiting For

The Seven Spiritual Laws
of Relationship: A Guide
to Growth and Happiness
for Couples on the Path
144 pages paperback $10.95
ISBN 1-879159-39-2

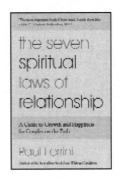

This simple but profound guide to growth and happiness
for couples will help you and your partner:

- Make a realistic commitment to one another
- Develop a shared experience that nurtures your relationship
- Give each other the space to grow and express yourselves as
  individuals
- Communicate by listening without judgment and telling the
  truth in a non-blaming way
- Understand how you mirror each other
- Stop blaming your partner and take responsibility for your
  thoughts, feelings and actions
- Practice forgiveness together on an ongoing basis

These seven spiritual principles will help you weather the
ups and downs of your relationship so that you and your partner can grow together and deepen the intimacy between you.
The book also includes a special section on living alone and
preparing to be in relationship and a section on separating
with love when a relationship needs to change form or come to
completion.

Our Surrender Invites Grace

Grace Unfolding: The Art of Living
A Surrendered Life
96 pages paperback $9.95
ISBN 1-879159-37-6

As we surrender to the truth of our being, we learn to relinquish the need to control our lives, figure things out, or predict the future. We begin to let go of our judgments and interpretations and accept life the way it is. When we can be fully present with whatever life brings, we are guided to take the next step on our journey. That is the way that grace unfolds in our lives.

Part IV of the Reflections of the Christ Mind Series is Hot off the Press

Return to the Garden
Reflections of The Christ Mind,
Part IV
$12.95, Paperback
ISBN # 1-879159-35-X

"In the Garden, all our needs were provided for. We knew no struggle or hardship. We were God's beloved. But happiness was not enough for us. We wanted the freedom to live our own lives. To evolve, we had to learn to become love-givers, not just love-receivers.

We all know what happened then. We were cast out of the Garden and for the first time in our lives we felt shame, jealousy, anger, lack. We experienced highs and lows, joy and sorrow. Our lives became difficult. We had to work hard to survive. We had to make mistakes and learn from them.

Initially, we tried to blame others for our mistakes. But that did not make our lives any easier. It just deepened our pain and misery. We had to learn to face our fears, instead of projecting them onto each other.

Returning to the Garden, we are different than we were when we left hellbent on expressing our creativity at any cost. We return humble and sensitive to the needs of all. We return not just as created, but as co-creator, not just as son of man, but also as son of God."

Learn the Spiritual Practice
Associated with the Christ Mind Teachings

**Living in the Heart
The Affinity Process
and the Path of
Unconditional Love
and Acceptance**
Paperback $10.95
ISBN 1-879159-36-8

The long awaited, definitive book on the *Affinity Process* is finally here. For years, the *Affinity Process* has been refined by participants so that it could be easily understood and experienced. Now, you can learn how to hold a safe, loving, non-judgmental space for yourself and others which will enable you to open your heart and move through your fears. The *Affinity Process* will help you learn to take responsibility for your fears and judgments so that you won't project them onto others. It will help you

129

learn to listen deeply and without judgment to others. And it will teach you how to tell your truth clearly without blaming others for your experience.

Part One contains an in-depth description of the principles on which the *Affinity Process* is based. Part Two contains a detailed discussion of the *Affinity Group* Guidelines. And Part Three contains a manual for people who wish to facilitate an *Affinity Group* in their community.

If you are a serious student of the Christ Mind teachings, this book is essential for you. It will enable you to begin a spiritual practice which will transform your life and the lives of others. It will also offer you a way of extending the teachings of love and forgiveness throughout your community.

Now Finally our Bestselling Title on Audio Tape

Love Without Conditions, Reflections of the Christ Mind, Part I by Paul Ferrini

The Book on Tape
Read by the Author
2 Cassettes,
Approximately 3.25 hours

ISBN 1-879159-24-4 $19.95

Now on audio tape: the incredible book from Jesus calling us to awaken to our own Christhood. Listen to this gentle, profound book while driving in your car or before going to sleep at night. Elisabeth Kubler-Ross calls this "the most important book I have read. I study it like a Bible." Find out for yourself how this amazing book has helped thousands of people understand the radical teachings of the master and begin to integrate these teachings into their lives.

Heartways Press
"Integrating Spirituality into Daily Life"
More Books by Paul Ferrini

With its heartfelt combination of sensuality and spirituality,
Paul Ferrini's poetry has been compared to the poetry of Rumi.

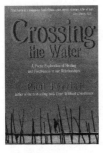

Crossing The Water
Poems About Healing and Forgiveness in
Our Relationships

*The time for healing and reconciliation has
come,* Ferrini writes. Our relationships help us
heal childhood wounds, walk through our deepest fears, and cross over the water of our
emotional pain. Just as the rocks in the river are *pounded and
caressed to rounded stone,* the rough edges of our personalities are
worn smooth in the context of a committed relationship. If we can
keep our hearts open, we can heal together, experience genuine
equality, and discover what it means to give and receive love without conditions.

With its heartfelt combination of sensuality and spirituality,
Paul Ferrini's poetry has been compared to the poetry of Rumi.
These luminous poems demonstrate why Paul Ferrini is first a
poet, a lover and a mystic. Come to this feast of the beloved with an
open heart and open ears. 96 pp. paper ISBN 1-879159-25-2
$9.95.

• Miracle of Love, Reflections of the Christ Mind, Part III

Many people say that this latest volume of the Christ Mind series is the best yet. Jesus tells us: "I was born to a simple woman in a barn. She was no more a virgin than your mother was." Moreover, he tells us, the virgin birth is not the only myth surrounding his life and teaching. So are the concepts of vicarious atonement and physical resurrection.

Relentlessly, the master tears down the rigid dogma and hierarchical teachings that obscure his simple message of love and forgiveness. He encourages us to take him down from the pedestal and the cross and see him as an equal brother who found the way out of suffering by opening his heart totally. We too can open our hearts and find peace and happiness. "The power of love will make miracles in your life as wonderful as any attributed to me," he tells us. "Your birth into this embodiment is no less holy than mine. The love that you extend to others is no less important than the love I extend to you." 192 pp. paper ISBN 1-879159-23-6 $12.95.

• Waking Up Together
Illuminations on the Road
to Nowhere

There comes a time for all of us when the outer destinations no longer satisfy and we finally understand that the love and happiness we seek cannot be found outside of us. It must be found in our own hearts, on the other side of our pain. "The Road to Nowhere is the path through your heart. It is not a journey of escape. It is a journey through your pain to end the pain of separation."

This book makes it clear that we can no longer rely on outer teachers or teachings to find our spiritual identity. Nor can we find who we are in relationships where boundaries are blurred and one person makes decisions for another. If we want to be authentic, we can't allow anyone else to be an authority for us, nor can we allow ourselves to be an authority for another person.

Authentic relationships happen between equal partners who take responsibility for their own consciousness and experience. When their buttons are pushed, they are willing to look at the obstacles they have erected to the experience of love and acceptance. As they understand and surrender the false ideas and emotional reactions that create separation, genuine intimacy becomes possible, and the sacred dimension of the relationship is born. 216 pp. paper ISBN 1-879159-17-1 $14.95

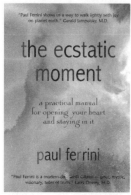

• **The Ecstatic Moment:**
A Practical Manual for Opening Your Heart and Staying in It.

A simple, power-packed guide that helps us take appropriate responsibility for our experience and establish healthy boundaries with others. Part II contains many helpful exercises and meditations that teach us to stay centered, clear and open in heart and mind. The Affinity Group Process and other group practices help us learn important listening and communication skills that can transform our troubled relationships. Once you have read this book, you will keep it in your briefcase or on your bedside table, referring to it often. You will not find a more practical, down to earth guide to contemporary spirituality. You will want to order copies for all your friends. 128 pp. paper ISBN 1-879159-18-X $10.95

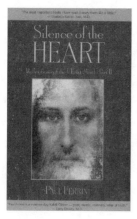

• **The Silence of the Heart**
Reflections of the Christ Mind,
Part II

A powerful sequel to *Love Without Conditions*. John Bradshaw says: "with deep insight and sparkling clarity, this book demonstrates that the roots of all abuse are to be found in our own self-betrayal. Paul Ferrini leads us skillfully and courageously beyond shame, blame, and attachment to our wounds into the depths of self-forgiveness. .a. must read for all people who are ready to take responsibility for their own healing." 218 pp. paper. ISBN 1-879159-16-3 $14.95

• Love Without Conditions:
Reflections of the Christ Mind, Part I

An incredible book from Jesus calling us to awaken to our Christhood. Rarely has any book conveyed the teachings of the master in such a simple but profound manner. This book will help you to bring your understanding from the head to the heart so that you can model the teachings of love and forgiveness in your daily life. 192 pp. paper ISBN 1-879159-15-15 $12.00

• The Wisdom of the Self

This ground-breaking book explores our authentic experience and our journey to wholeness. "Your life is your spiritual path. Don't be quick to abandon it for promises of bigger and better experiences. You are getting exactly the experiences you need to grow. If your growth seems too slow or uneventful for you, it is because you have not fully embraced the situations and relationships at hand. .To know the Self is to allow everything, to embrace the totality of who we are, all that we think and feel, all of our fear, all of our love." 229 pp. paper ISBN 1-879159-14-7 $12.00

• The Twelve Steps of Forgiveness

A practical manual for healing ourselves and our relationships. This book gives us a step-by-step process for moving through our fears, projections, judgments, and guilt so that we can take responsibility for creating the life we want. With great gentleness, we learn to embrace our lessons and to find equality with others. A must read for all in recovery and others seeking spiritual wholeness. 128 pp. paper ISBN 1-879159-10-4 $10.00

• The Wounded Child's Journey Into Love's Embrace

This book explores a healing process in which we confront our deep-seated guilt and fear, bringing love and forgiveness to the wounded child within. By surrendering our judgments of self and others, we overcome feelings of separation and dismantle co-dependent patterns that restrict our self-expression and ability to give and receive love. 225pp. paper ISBN 1-879159-06-6 $12.00

• The Bridge to Reality

A Heart-Centered Approach to *A Course in Miracles* and the Process of Inner Healing. Sharing his experiences of spiritual awakening, Paul emphasizes self-acceptance and forgiveness as cornerstones of spiritual practice. Presented with beautiful photos, this book conveys the essence of *The Course* as it is lived in daily life. 192 pp. paper ISBN 1-879159-03-1 $12.00

• From Ego to Self

108 illustrated affirmations designed to offer you a new way of viewing conflict situations so that you can overcome negative thinking and bring more energy, faith and optimism into your life. 144 pp. paper ISBN 1-879159-01-5 $10.00

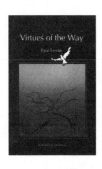

• Virtues of The Way

A lyrical work of contemporary scripture reminiscent of the Tao Te Ching. Beautifully illustrated, this inspirational book will help you cultivate the spiritual values required to fulfill your creative purpose and live in harmony with others. 64 pp. paper ISBN 1-879159-02-3 $7.50

• The Body of Truth

A crystal clear introduction to the universal teachings of love and forgiveness. This book traces all forms of suffering to negative attitudes and false beliefs, which we have the ability to transform. 64 pp. paper ISBN 1-879159-02-3 $7.50

• Available Light

Inspirational, passionate poems dealing with the work of inner integration, love and relationships, death and re-birth, loss and abundance, life purpose and the reality of spiritual vision. 128 pp. paper ISBN 1-879159-05-8 $12.00

Poetry and Guided Meditation Tapes
by Paul Ferrini

The Poetry of the Soul

With its heartfelt combination of sensuality and spirituality, Paul Ferrini's poetry has been compared to the poetry of Rumi. These luminous poems demonstrate why Paul Ferrini is first a poet, a lover and a mystic. Come to this feast of the beloved with an open heart and open ears. With Suzi Kesler on piano. $10.00 ISBN 1-879159-26-0

The Circle of Healing

The meditation and healing tape that many of you have been seeking. This gentle meditation opens the heart to love's presence and extends that love to all the beings in your experience. A powerful tape with inspirational piano accompaniment by Michael Gray. ISBN 1-879159-08-2 $10.00

Healing the Wounded Child

A potent healing tape that accesses old feelings of pain, fragmentation, self-judgment and separation and brings them into the light of conscious awareness and acceptance. Side two includes a hauntingly beautiful "inner child" reading from *The Bridge to Reality* with piano accompaniment by Michael Gray. ISBN 1-879159-11-2 $10.00

Forgiveness: Returning to the Original Blessing

A self healing tape that helps us accept and learn from the mistakes we have made in the past. By letting go of our judgments and ending our ego-based search for perfection, we can bring our darkness to the light, dissolving anger, guilt, and shame. Piano accompaniment by Michael Gray. ISBN 1-879159-12-0 $10.00

Paul Ferrini Talks and Workshop Tapes

Answering Our Own Call for Love *A Sermon given at the Pacific Church of Religious Science in San Diego, CA November, 1997*

Paul tells the story of his own spiritual awakening, his Atheist upbringing, and how he began to open to the presence of God and his connection with Jesus and the Christ Mind teaching. In a very clear, heartfelt way, Paul presents to us the spiritual path of love, acceptance, and forgiveness. Also available on videotape. 1 Cassette *$10.00 ISBN 1-879159-33-3*

The Ecstatic Moment *A workshop given by Paul in Los Angeles at the Agape International Center of Truth, May, 1997*

Shows us how we can be with our pain compassionately and learn to nurture the light within ourselves, even when it appears that we are walking through darkness. Discusses subjects such as living in the present, acceptance, not fixing self or others, being with our discomfort and learning that we are lovable as we are. *1 Cassette $10.00 ISBN 1-879159-27-9*

Honoring Self and Other *A Workshop at the Pacific Church of Religious Science in San Diego, November, 1997*

Helps us understand the importance of not betraying ourselves in our relationships with others. Focuses on understanding healthy boundaries, setting limits, and saying no to others in a loving way. Real life examples include a woman who is married to a man who is chronically critical of her, and a gay man who wants to tell his judgmental parents that he has AIDS. *1 Cassette $10.00 ISBN 1-879159-34-1*

Seek First the Kingdom *Two Sunday Messages given by Paul: the first in May, 1997 in Los Angeles at the Agape Int'l. Center of Truth, and the second in September, 1997 in Portland, OR at the Unity Church.*

Discusses the words of Jesus in the Sermon on the Mount: "Seek first the kingdom and all else will be added to you." Helps us understand how we create the inner temple by learning to hold our judgments of self and other more compassionately. The love of God flows through our love and acceptance of ourselves. As we establish our connection to the divine within ourselves, we don't need to look outside of ourselves for love and acceptance. Includes fabulous music by The Agape Choir and Band. *1 Cassette $10.00 ISBN 1-879159-30-9*

Double Cassette Tape Sets

Ending the Betrayal of the Self *A Workshop given by Paul at the Learning Annex in Toronto, April, 1997*

A roadmap for integrating the opposing voices in our psyche so that we can experience our own wholeness. Delineates what our responsibility is and isn't in our relationships with others, and helps us learn to set clear, firm, but loving boundaries. Our relationships can become areas of sharing and fulfillment, rather than mutual invitations to co-dependency and self betrayal. *2 Cassettes $16.95 ISBN 1-879159-28-7*

140

Relationships: Changing Past Patterns *A Talk with Questions and Answers Given at the Redondo Beach Church of Religious Science, 11/97*

Begins with a Christ Mind talk describing the link between learning to love and accept ourselves and learning to love and accept others. Helps us understand how we are invested in the past and continue to replay our old relationship stories. Helps us get clear on what we want and understand how to be faithful to it. By being totally committed to ourselves, we give birth to the beloved within and also without. Includes an in-depth discussion about meditation, awareness, hearing our inner voice, and the Affinity Group Process. *2 Cassettes $16.95 ISBN 1-879159-32-5*

Relationship As a Spiritual Path *A workshop given by Paul in Los Angeles at the Agape Int'l. Center of Truth, May, 1997*

Explores concrete ways in which we can develop a relationship with ourselves and learn to take responsibility for our own experience, instead of blaming others for our perceived unworthiness. Also discussed: accepting our differences, the new paradigm of relationship, the myth of the perfect partner, telling our truth, compassion vs. rescuing, the unavailable partner, abandonment issues, negotiating needs, when to say no, when to stay and work on a relationship and when to leave. *2 Cassettes $16.95 ISBN 1-879159-29-5*

Opening to Christ Consciousness *A Talk with Questions & Answers at Unity Church, Tustin, CA November, 1997*

Begins with a Christ Mind talk giving us a clear picture of how the divine spark dwells within each of us and how we can open up to God-consciousness on a regular basis. Deals with letting go and forgiveness in our relationships with our parents, our children and our partners. A joyful, funny, and scintillating tape you will want to listen to many times. Also available on videotape. *2 Cassettes $16.95 ISBN 1-879159-31-7*

Risen Christ Posters and Notecards

11"x17" Poster
suitable for framing
ISBN 1-879159-19-8 $10.00

Set of 8 Notecards
with Envelopes
ISBN 1-879159-20-1 $10.00

Ecstatic Moment Posters and Notecards

8.5"x11" Poster
suitable for framing
ISBN 1-879159-21-X $5.00

Set of 8 Notecards
with Envelopes
ISBN 1-879159-22-8 $10.00

Heartways Press Order Form

Name_____

Address_____

City _____State _____Zip _____

Phone _____

BOOKS BY PAUL FERRINI

The Seven Spiritual Laws of Relationship ($10.95) _____

Grace Unfolding: The Art of Living A Surrendered Life ($9.95) _____

Return to the Garden ($12.95) _____

Living in the Heart ($10.95) _____

Miracle of Love ($12.95) _____

Crossing the Water ($9.95) _____

Waking Up Together ($14.95) _____

The Ecstatic Moment ($10.95) _____

The Silence of the Heart ($14.95) _____

Love Without Conditions ($12.00) _____

The Wisdom of the Self ($12.00) _____

The Twelve Steps of Forgiveness ($10.00) _____

The Circle of Atonement ($12.00) _____

The Bridge to Reality ($12.00) _____

From Ego to Self ($10.00) _____

Virtues of the Way ($7.50) _____

The Body of Truth ($7.50) _____

Available Light ($10.00) _____

AUDIO TAPES BY PAUL FERRINI

The Circle of Healing ($10.00) _____

Healing the Wounded Child ($10.00) _____

Forgiveness: Returning to the Original Blessing ($10.00) _____

The Poetry of the Soul ($10.00) _____

Seek First the Kingdom ($10.00) _____

Answering Our Own Call for Love ($10.00) _____

The Ecstatic Moment ($10.00) _____

Honoring Self and Other ($10.00) _____

Love Without Conditions ($19.95) 2 tapes _____

Ending the Betrayal of the Self ($16.95) 2 tapes _____

Relationships: Changing Past Patterns ($16.95) 2 tapes _____

Relationship As a Spiritual Path ($16.95) 2 tapes _____

Opening to Christ Consciousness ($16.95) 2 tapes _____

Continued on Backside

POSTERS AND NOTECARDS

Risen Christ Poster 11"x17" ($10.00)   ____

Ecstatic Moment Poster 8.5"x11" ($5.00)   ____

Risen Christ Notecards with envelopes 8/pkg ($10.00)   ____

Ecstatic Moment Notecards with envelopes 8/pkg ($10.00)   ____

SHIPPING

($2.00 for first item, $1.00 each additional item.
Add additional $1.00 for first class postage.)   ____
MA residents please add 5% sales tax.   ____

TOTAL $ ____

Please allow 1-2 weeks for delivery

Send Order To: Heartways Press
P. O. Box 181, South Deerfield, MA 01373
413-665-0555 • 413-665-4565 (fax)
Toll free: 1-888-HARTWAY (Orders only)